African Americans
Their Impact on U.S. History

by
Doris Hunter Metcalf

illustrated by Paul Manktelow

Cover by Ted Warren

Copyright © Good Apple, 1992

ISBN No. 0-86653-670-1

Printing No. 987654

Good Apple
1204 Buchanan St., Box 299
Carthage, IL 62321-0299

SIMON & SCHUSTER *A Paramount Communications Company*

Table of Contents

Dedication

To James and Bessie Hunter
For their love and inspiration

To the Teacher

American history is a history of a great nation and its people—*all of its people*. Therefore it should be presented and studied as the combined efforts of all Americans who helped to make it great. But for many years the role that African Americans played in the development of this country has been largely ignored.

African Americans: Their Impact on U.S. History is designed to provide the opportunity for all students to learn the roles of African Americans in the development of American history. It presents the roles of African Americans during ten major historical eras: the Colonial, the Revolutionary War, the Abolition Movement, the Civil War, Reconstruction, the Spanish-American War, World War I, the Great Depression, World War II and the Civil Rights Era. Each era contains historical information pages followed by related activity pages of stimulating activities to increase reading comprehension skills and to improve creative thinking and research skills.

Some of the greatest historical events in American history have involved African Americans. *African Americans: Their Impact on U.S. History* provides the classroom teacher with readily accessible information for the inclusion of the roles of African Americans during the study of major historical events in American history.

African Americans: Their Impact on U.S. History can be included in the curriculum whenever major historical events are studied, or it can be used in a learning center setting to provide meaningful learning experiences for those students who finish regular classroom work early. *African Americans: Their Impact on U.S. History* can also be used as an independent learning project for fast learners.

A greater awareness of African Americans' role in the development of American history will undoubtedly lead to a better understanding of American history and a greater appreciation for all of its people.

What's in a Name?

In early American history, Black Americans were referred to as "colored." Even well into the 1950's and 1960's, signs above water fountains, bathrooms, restaurants and other public places designated Black Americans as "colored." But Black Americans then preferred the name Negro. They felt that the name "colored" did not properly represent them and that it was a name given to them by White Americans. Therefore it was despised. Their preferred name "Negro" was often mispronounced on purpose in order to degrade Black Americans.

Later, Negroes began to refer to themselves as Black Americans. This name they felt better described them. In the 1950's and 1960's Black Americans began to develop a pride in their heritage. They selected the name Afro-American to reflect their African origin. They adopted the slogan "I am black and I am proud." Along with the name change, Black Americans adopted a new hairstyle. It was called an afro. With the afro, the hair was allowed to grow and curl naturally into a bushy hairstyle. Clothing styles also changed a bit. The Dashiki, an African loose-fitting shirt, became a popular style especially for young Black American men.

In the later part of the 1960's a group of young Black Americans grew tired of using the nonviolent approach to solving their problems. They were called Black Militants. They formed groups such as the Black Panthers. The Black Panthers urged Black Americans to gain control of schools and businesses in their communities. They believed in meeting violence with violence. The Black Panthers wore black jackets and berets. Their salute was a raised clenched fist. Their chant was "Power to the People." Many young Black Americans liked the Panthers' style of behavior and dress. One of the heroes of the Panthers was a Black Muslim leader called Malcolm X. Malcolm X was born Malcolm Little. He believed that his last name had been given to his ancestors by their slave master, so he dropped his last name and placed an X there instead. The X meant that his real last name was unknown. When the Black Muslim Movement began to spread, other Black Americans began changing their names too. Cassius Clay, the famous Black American, changed his name to Muhammad Ali. In the 1980's and the 1990's Black Americans chose other names for themselves. Their new name is African Americans. They feel that this name reflects their past as well as their present.

Today many Black Americans choose African names for their children. They want them to always remember their African heritage and to be proud of it.

GA1345

The Colonial Era

During the 1600's many Europeans wanted to come to the American colonies for a better life, but many of these Europeans were poor and did not have the money for the trip to the New World. In exchange for the price of a trip, many agreed to become servants to wealthy landowners for a period of five to seven years. The servants were called indentured servants. When the agreed term was over, the indentured servants were free to begin new lives.

In 1619, one year before the landing of the Pilgrims and twelve years after the founding of the Jamestown colony in Virginia, a Dutch ship brought twenty Africans as indentured servants to the Virginia colony. The colonists had thought that white indentured servants and Native Americans could supply all of their labor needs, but by the end of the seventeenth century, the colonies began growing large plantation crops of cotton and tobacco. These plantation crops were sold to England for goods that the colonies needed. As more colonies began to grow and export more crops, more workers were needed to work the crops. In 1793 the cotton gin was invented. This machine made it much easier to process large amounts of cotton. The high demand for cotton led plantation owners to grow larger crops of cotton. These large crops required many more workers. In order to provide workers to grow and gather these crops, thousands of Africans were captured in their homeland of Africa and brought to the colonies against their will. They were sold to plantation owners and slave trading had begun in the United States.

Being a slave meant being under the complete control of someone else. A slave was owned by a master who gave him just enough food and clothing to keep him working in the fields. A slave did not have any rights. He could not own property. In fact, a slave was property himself. He could be bought, sold or traded. Many times an entire family would be torn apart during an auction or sale. A mother might be bought by one slave master, the father by another and the children by still another. In the Southern colonies slaves worked in cotton, rice and tobacco fields. In the Northern colonies they worked as carpenters, blacksmiths, clerks and sailors.

Slave trading became a big business. Slave ownership became a sign of wealth and power among Southern plantation owners.

With steady importation, the slave population grew quickly from a few hundred to thousands. There were no laws as to how slaves should be treated. So the colonies made their own laws. These laws were called Black Codes. They were strict laws that regulated the life of a slave. Under the Black Codes, a slave could not own a gun or any kind of weapon or ammunition. Slaves could not assemble in large groups for fear of an uprising or revolt. A slave was not free to go where he wanted to go. Special permission from his master was required in order for a slave to visit another community. A slave was forbidden to learn to read or write.

Slavery first began in the Virginia colony but soon spread to other states. It lasted over 200 years. During this time over 15 million African Americans were sold into slavery and over 35 million lost their lives in the process.

GA1345

Unlock It!

Write the answers to the statements on the locks in the matching keys. Use words from the word vault.

Africa	Word Vault		Northern colonies
slaves	Black Codes	southern colonies	cotton gin
indentured servant	auction	master	slave ownership

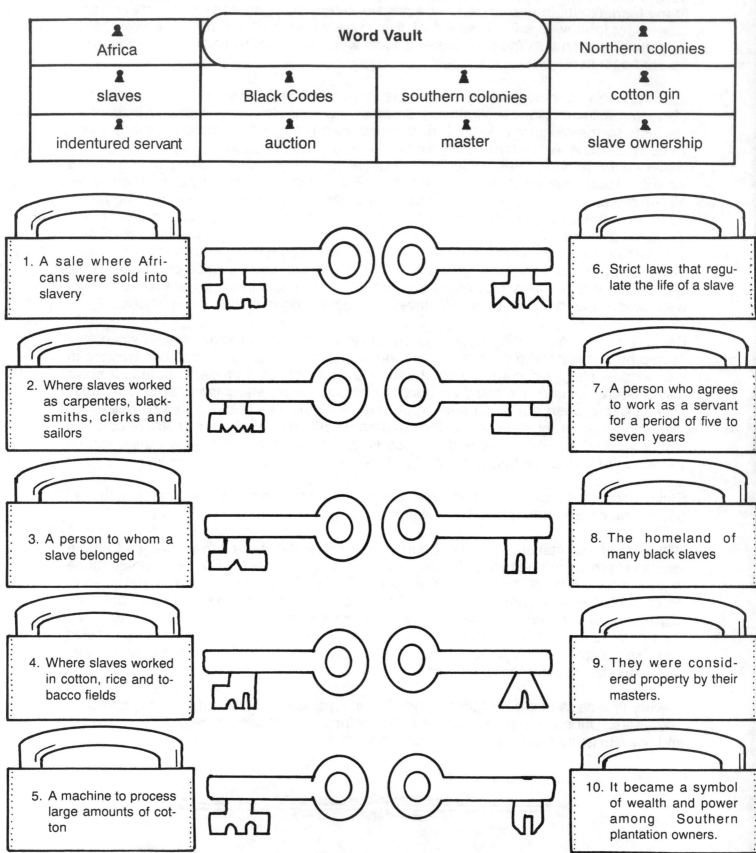

1. A sale where Africans were sold into slavery

2. Where slaves worked as carpenters, blacksmiths, clerks and sailors

3. A person to whom a slave belonged

4. Where slaves worked in cotton, rice and tobacco fields

5. A machine to process large amounts of cotton

6. Strict laws that regulate the life of a slave

7. A person who agrees to work as a servant for a period of five to seven years

8. The homeland of many black slaves

9. They were considered property by their masters.

10. It became a symbol of wealth and power among Southern plantation owners.

GA1345

The Solomon Northrup Case

During the Colonial Era, some slave owners were kind to their slaves. But others were very harsh. Many slaves were disgusted and tired of being mistreated by their masters. Many found the courage to run away from their masters. In 1850 the Fugitive Slave Law was enacted. Under this law runaway slaves could be captured and returned to their owners. Orders were issued and wanted posters were displayed for each escaped slave. Sometimes free Africans were captured in the North and sold as slaves to the South. Such was the case of Solomon Northrup. Solomon Northrup was born a free man in New York in the year 1808. When he grew up and married, he settled in Saratoga Springs, New York. Both Solomon and his wife Anne worked at the United States Hotel in New York. He played the violin and drove a horse cab while his wife Anne worked as a cook.

One spring day in 1841, two white men were passing through Saratoga Springs. They heard Solomon playing his violin. They pretended to be owners of a circus and told Solomon that he would be paid well if he would come with them to play the violin in Washington, D.C. When they reached Washington, D.C., Solomon was drugged and sold as a slave. When Solomon awoke, he learned that he had been sold as a slave. He tried to explain this to his new master, but his new master would not listen. He had been bought for a good price, and the new master was not about to let him go. As is often the case, Solomon was sold again, this time to a plantation owner in Louisiana, where he lived for twelve years as a plantation slave. Through hard work and harsh treatment, Solomon never gave up his idea of returning to his family. One day Solomon finally found someone to help him. A white plantation owner listened to Solomon's story. Samuel Bass contacted a lawyer in New York who worked with a lawyer in Louisiana. They helped Solomon regain his freedom. Solomon was freed and returned to his wife and children in New York. Solomon had served twelve years as a slave. After his arrival in New York, he returned to Washington D.C., to bring charges against those who had captured him. When the case went to court, the two white men who had captured Solomon claimed that he had been exchanged to them to pay a gambling debt. The court believed them and dismissed the case. The men were never punished for their evil deed.

Solomon Northrup was a fortunate man to be reunited with his family and to be a free man again. Many other free men were not so fortunate. Many of them were captured and sold into slavery, there to live and die without ever seeing their families again.

In 1853, Solomon wrote a book about his life as a slave. The book was entitled *Twelve Years a Slave*. It told of all of the hardship that he had suffered while being a slave.

GA1345

Write It!

Write ten facts about the life of Solomon Northrup in the open pages of the book below.

Write the title of Solomon Northrup's book on the illustration below. Then use markers or crayons and design a cover.

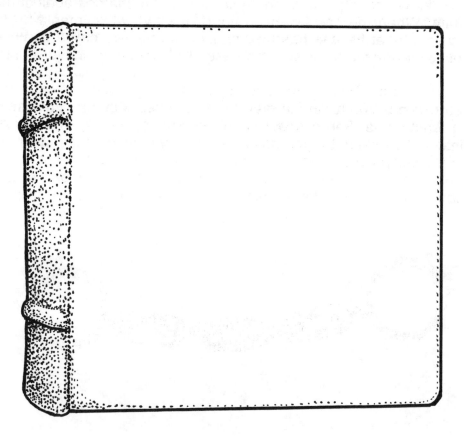

The Life of a Slave

Josiah Henson was born a slave in the state of Maryland in 1789. When he was a young child, his mother was beaten by a cruel overseer, a person who was hired by the slave owner to watch over the slaves as they worked. When Josiah's father tried to stop the overseer, he was beaten too. The overseer reported the incident to the slave owner, who quickly sold Josiah's mother and father leaving Josiah an orphan. When Josiah grew up he worked long hours as a field hand. One day his master told him that he had been a very hard worker and that he was going to trust him to be an overseer of other slaves. Josiah earned the trust of his master. Once he was sent to Kentucky to deliver some slaves to another slave owner. He worked there in Kentucky for three years. When he had earned enough money, he returned to his master to buy his freedom. Josiah had been such an honest worker and so trustworthy that the master would not let him go. After several attempts to buy his freedom, the slave owner became angry and told Josiah that he was becoming a troublemaker and that he was going to sell him "down the river." This meant that he would be sold to a cruel and harsh owner. When Josiah learned of his master's plans, he began to make plans of his own. Josiah thought "I have been the best worker that I could be, and this is the thanks that I get. I only want to buy my freedom." Josiah did not know what to do. Finally the thought entered his mind—escape! Escape!

Josiah and his wife and children made careful plans, and when the time was right, Josiah and his family escaped to Ohio then on to Canada, where he joined the workers on the underground railroad.

Later, during his lifetime, he wrote of his experience as a field hand slave. He gave a firsthand account of his life as a slave. He said that he wore clothing made of towel cloth and that he had one pair of coarse shoes to last all year. He lived in a one-room hut without floors or windows. His entire family of ten or twelve persons all crammed into this one large room. The beds were made of piles of straw and old rags in a corner of the room. In the winter cold wind, rain and snow would fall through large cracks in the ceiling. Sometimes when it rained a lot the floor would become as muddy as a pigpen.

Josiah would work in the fields from sunup to sundown, stopping only a few minutes for a lunch of cold bread. When the fieldwork was over he helped with household chores, ate a meal of bread and water and went to take his place among his other family members on his bed of straw and rags. Sleep did not come easy, but Josiah knew that he had to get some sleep because at the crack of dawn he would have to be up and off to the fields again.

GA1345

Picture This

Use your imagination and Josiah's descriptions in "The Life of a Slave," to draw the following items:

clothing made of towel cloth

one pair of coarse shoes

one-room log hut

bed of straw and old rags

Pretend that your house was part of the underground railroad where Josiah Henson stopped on his way to freedom in the North. On the back of your paper, sketch the floor plan of your house or apartment and place an *X* to show a good place where a runaway slave might hide. Then tell why you chose the place you did.

Place It

Directions

Place a number beside each statement to show the sequence of events in the life of Josiah Henson. Use numbers 1-15.

_____ Josiah and his wife escaped to Ohio.

_____ Josiah's mother was beaten by a cruel overseer.

_____ Josiah, his wife and children went to Canada.

_____ Josiah was born a slave in Maryland.

_____ Josiah earned the trust of his master.

_____ The overseer reported Josiah's father to the slave owner.

_____ Josiah had been so trustworthy that his master would not let him go.

_____ The slave owner told Josiah that he would be sold "down the river."

_____ Josiah's father tried to stop the overseer from beating his mother.

_____ Josiah's mother and father were sold, leaving Josiah an orphan.

_____ Josiah was sent to Kentucky to deliver some slaves.

_____ When Josiah heard of his master's plans, he began to make plans of his own.

_____ Josiah returned to his master to buy his freedom.

_____ Finally the thought entered Josiah's mind—escape! Escape!

_____ Josiah spent three years in Kentucky.

Freedom Certificate (Part 1)

You are a slave during the Colonial Era in America. You have a chance to earn your freedom if you can complete these requirements. Answer the questions below. Write your answers in the space following each question.

1. Name two free African Americans who established churches and other organizations.

   _____

2. Who was Anthony Johnson? _____

3. What were some of the rights that free African Americans had by the year 1790? __

   _____

4. How did the status of free African Americans change before the Civil War? _____

   _____

5. Write a biography of a famous African American in American history in the space below.

   _____

   _____

   _____

   _____

   _____

   _____

   _____

   _____

   _____

   _____

   _____

   _____

   _____

   _____

   _____

   _____

   _____

GA1345

Freedom Certificate (Part 2)

This is your Freedom Certificate. Complete it and keep it with you at all times.

Name _____ Age _____

Date of Birth _____ Sex (male/female) _____

Height _____ Weight _____

Hair Color _____ Eye Color _____

In the space below name as many certificates and/or licenses that you can think of. One has been given for you.

1. Fishing license
2. _____
3. _____
4. _____
5. _____
6. _____
7. _____
8. _____
9. _____
10. _____
11. _____
12. _____
13. _____
14. _____
15. _____
16. _____
17. _____
18. _____
19. _____
20. _____
21. _____
22. _____
23. _____
24. _____
25. _____

26. _____
27. _____
28. _____
29. _____
30. _____
31. _____
32. _____
33. _____
34. _____
35. _____
36. _____
37. _____
38. _____
39. _____
40. _____
41. _____
42. _____
43. _____
44. _____
45. _____
46. _____
47. _____
48. _____
49. _____
50. _____

GA1345

Three Who Tried

O' freedom! O' freedom!
O' freedom over me!
An' befo' I'd be a slave,
I'll be buried in my grave,
An' go home to my Lord an' be free.

These words are taken from a slave song sung in the early colonial days. They tell of the desire of the slave to be free. Many slaves were willing to risk their lives for freedom.

During the colonial years, hundreds of attempts were made by slaves to free themselves. These "*tries*" or attempts to escape were called *slave revolts* or *slave uprisings*.

More than 400 slave revolts took place between 1750 and 1850. Some slaves rebelled against harsh treatments by hurting themselves. They broke their own legs or cut off their fingers or hands to make themselves useless to their masters. Many slaves plotted secretly to kill their masters and escape to the North.

During the summer of 1800 a slave named Gabriel Prosser planned a daring slave revolt. He sent word to other slaves throughout the plantations in Henrico County, Virginia, that they should all rise up against their masters on August 30th. More than 10,000 slaves were secretly told about the revolt. They began to make preparations. Things went well until the day of the revolt. On that day a great wind and rainstorm kept the slaves from assembling and two slaves betrayed Prosser and revealed the plans of the revolt to their masters. Word passed quickly to slave owners and then to Governor James Monroe (he became the fifth President of the United States). Governor Monroe broke up the plot. Gabriel and thirty of his leaders were tried and hanged during the months of September and October of 1800.

In 1922 one of the largest slave revolts in the history of the United States was planned by a former slave named Denmark Vessey. It involved slaves in Charleston, South Carolina, and the surrounding area. Thousands of slaves were involved, but the exact details were never revealed. Those who were involved had taken an oath to "seal their lips and die in silence." Even though he did not know the details, a slave informer revealed the plot to his master. Denmark Vessey and his leaders were arrested and later hanged. The slave informer was given a pension of $50 a year by the state of South Carolina. In 1857 the pension was raised to $200 a year.

One of the best-known slave revolts that was never forgotten by the South was the one led by Nat Turner. He stated that he had a vision and that he had been called to take up arms against slave owners and free his people.

He led a revolt in Southampton County, Virginia. No one betrayed him and no one revealed his plans. On August 22, 1831, Nat Turner and a group of twelve fellow slaves armed themselves with hatchets and axes and went on a rampage of slaughter on slave masters to give freedom to their slaves. Within thirty-six hours over sixty slave masters, including Nat Turner's master and his entire family, were killed and their slaves freed. His plans were to continue to kill slave masters and free their slaves, but his plans had to be discontinued. In time, the revolt became known and federal and state troops were sent to control the revolt. Nat Turner and seventeen of his leaders were captured and hanged.

The Nat Turner revolt struck terror into the heart of every southern slave master. They lived in constant fear of future revolts. To prevent this, several states passed laws called Black Codes. These laws regulated and controlled the lives of the slaves. They placed restrictions on the travel and gathering of slaves. But the Nat Turner revolt could not be undone. It was one that the South would always remember.

GA1345

You Try

Directions
Fill in the chart with the correct information.

Name of Slave	Year of Revolt	Place of Revolt	Reasons the Revolt Failed
Gabriel Prosser			
Denmark Vessey			
Nat Turner			

Use an encyclopedia or other reference book to read about the Toussaint L'ouverture Revolt. Write some information from your reading in the space below.

_____

_____

_____

_____

_____

_____

_____

_____

_____

_____

_____

_____

_____

_____

_____

_____

_____

_____

They Sang Spirituals

While working on the plantations (large cotton, tobacco or sugarcane farms) slaves sang spirituals to help them bear the burden of hard work and long working hours. These beautiful songs and music have made a great contribution to the world of music.

Slave children owned only one pair of shoes that was to last all year. To help them express hope for a better life with more than one pair of shoes, they sang:
> I got shoes, you've got shoes,
> All God's children got shoes.
> When I get to heaven, gonna put on my shoes
> Gonna shout all over God's heaven.

When the slaves longed for freedom they hoped for a "Moses" to deliver them from bondage, they sang:
> When Israel was in Egypt's land,
> Let my people go;
> Oppressed so hard they could not stand,
> Let my people go.
> Go down, Moses,
> Way down in Egypt's land,
> Tell ole pharaoh,
> Let my people go.

In this spiritual, the pharaoh was the slave master, Moses was the conductor on the underground railroad and the people were the slaves.

On some occasions the words of certain spirituals were used as "code" words to signal escapes, revolts or secret meetings. To signal other slaves to come to a secret meeting, a slave might sing:
> Steal away, steal away,
> Steal away to Jesus,
> Steal away home,
> I ain't got long to stay here.

Songs like "Swing Low, Sweet Chariot" would give slaves the hope of an escape on the underground railroad. They would sing:
> Swing low, sweet chariot,
> Coming for to carry me home,
> Swing low, sweet chariot,
> Coming for to carry me home.

When Harriet Tubman made trips to the South to help slaves escape to freedom in the North, she would signal to the slaves with a coded song called "Follow the Drinking Gourd." Softly and secretly, she sang to the waiting slaves:
> Follow, follow, follow
> Follow the drinking gourd,
> Follow the drinking gourd;
> For the old man is a-waiting for to carry you to freedom
> If you follow the drinking gourd.

A drinking gourd was a dried vegetable shaped like a dipper that was used in the slaves' households to dip water from a bucket for drinking. In the spiritual, the drinking gourd represented the Big Dipper—a group of stars arranged in the shape of a dipper in the northern sky. The North Star is one of the stars that forms the Little Dipper. Escaping slaves used it to find their way to the North.

To those who did not understand, a spiritual was just another song, but to the slave, a spiritual had a special meaning. Slaves could sing their spirituals anywhere because their masters were not aware of the songs' special meanings. They thought the slaves sang because they were happy.

GA1345

Star Search

The Big Dipper is a constellation. A constellation is a group of stars that forms special shapes in the sky. By knowing the position of constellations, it is possible to locate other stars. There are more than eighty constellations. They include the twelve zodiac signs as well as other star groups. Can you locate twenty constellations in the puzzle below?

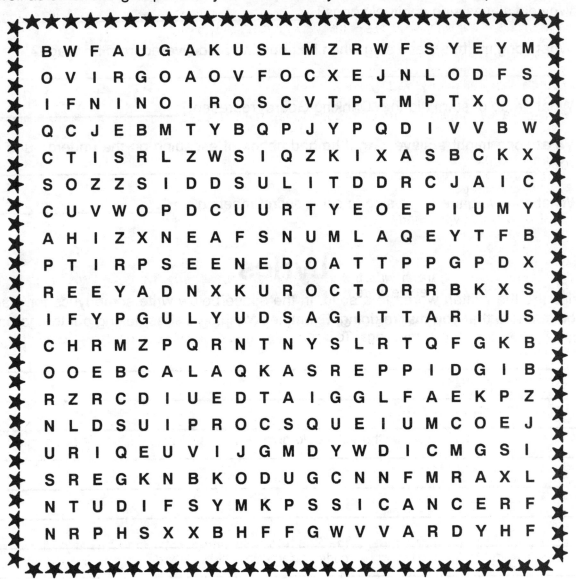

```
B W F A U G A K U S L M Z R W F S Y E Y M
O V I R G O A O V F O C X E J N L O D F S
I F N I N O I R O S C V T P T M P T X O O
Q C J E B M T Y B Q P J Y P Q D I V V B W
C T I S R L Z W S I Q Z K I X A S B C K X
S O Z Z S I D D S U L I T D D R C J A I C
C U V W O P D C U U R T Y E O E P I U M Y
A H I Z X N E A F S N U M L A Q E Y T F B
P T I R P S E E N E D O A T T P P G P D X
R E E Y A D N X K U R O C T O R R B K X S
I F Y P G U L Y U D S A G I T T A R I U S
C H R M Z P Q R N T N Y S L R T Q F G K B
O O E B C A L A Q K A S R E P P I D G I B
R Z R C D I U E D T A I G G L F A E K P Z
N L D S U I P R O C S Q U E I U M C O E J
U R I Q E U V I J G M D Y W D I C M G S I
S R E G K N B K O D U G C N N F M R A X L
N T U D I F S Y M K P S S I C A N C E R F
N R P H S X X B H F F G W V V A R D Y H F
```

Can you find these words?

Little Dipper	Sagittarius	Capricornus
Cassiopeia	Big Dipper	Andromeda
Eridanus	Aquarius	Scorpius
Hercules	Cancer	Gemini
Taurus	Pisces	Hydra
Aries	Libra	Virgo
Orion	Leo	

13

GA1345

Answer, Please!

Directions
Fill in the blanks with the correct answers.

1. Why did slaves sing spiritual songs? _____

2. What song might a slave sing when he hoped to be delivered from bondage?

_____

3. What group of stars did the "Drinking Gourd" represent? _____

4. What song might a slave sing if he had hopes of escaping on the underground railroad?_____

5. What song might a slave sing to call a secret meeting? _____

Lyrics

Lyrics are the written words to a song. In the space below write some lyrics for a song about a chore that you dislike doing. Example: Washing dishes, taking out the garbage, etc.

_____

_____

_____

_____

_____

_____

_____

_____

_____

_____

_____

_____

_____

_____

GA1345

Choral Reading

Directions

Organize the class into two groups. Have each group speak the lines as indicated below. The chorus should be read after each verse.

Go Down, Moses

Verse 1

Group 1	When Israel was in Egypt's land,
Group 2	Let my people go;
Group 1	Oppressed so hard they could not stand,
Group 2	Let my people go.

Chorus

Group 1	Go down, Moses, way down in Egypt's land,
Group 2	Tell ole pharaoh,
Group 1	Let my people go.

Verse 2

Group 2	No more shall they in bondage toil,
Group 1	Let my people go;
Group 2	Let them come out with Egypt's spoil,
Group 1	Let my people go.

Verse 3

Group 2	The Lord told Moses what to do,
Group 1	Let my people go;
Group 2	To lead the children of Egypt through,
Group 1	Let my people go.

Verse 4

Group 2	When they had reached the other shore,
Group 1	Let my people go;
Group 2	They sang a song of triumph o'er,
Group 1	Let my people go.

Verse 5

Group 2	O' let us all for bondage flee,
Group 1	Let my people go;
Group 2	And let us all in Christ be free,
Group 1	Let my people go.

GA1345

Decode It!

Directions

Use the alphabet code to decode the titles of some well-known spiritual songs.

A	B	C	D	E	F	G	H	I	J	K	L	M	N	O	P	Q	R	S	T	U	V	W	X	Y	Z
1	2	3	4	5	6	7	8	9	10	11	12	13	14	15	16	17	18	19	20	21	22	23	24	25	26

Songs

1. "___ ___ ___ ___ ___ ___ ___ ___ ___ ___ , ___ ___ ___ ___ ___ ___
    7 5 20   15 14   2 15 1 18 4   12 9 20 20 12 5

  ___ ___ ___ ___ ___ ___ ___ ___ "
   3 8 9 12 4 18 5 14

2. "___ ___ ' ___ ___ ___ , ___ ___ ___ ___ ___ ___ "
   9 20 19   13 5   15 8   12 15 18 4

3. "___ ___ ___ ___ ___ ___ ___ ___ ___ "
   4 5 5 16   18 9 22 5 18

4. "___ ___ ___ ___ ___ ___ ___ ___ "
   7 18 5 1 20   4 1 25

5. "___ ___ ___ ___ ___ ___ ___ , ___ ___ ___ ___ ___ ___ ___ ___ ___ ___
   3 15 21 12 4 14 20   8 5 1 18   14 15 2 15 4 25

  ___ ___ ___ ___ "
  16 18 1 25

16

GA1345

The Drinking Gourd Game

Materials: Playing pieces, playing cards, paper die, gameboard, encyclopedia or other reference books on African history

Object: To be the first to reach Safety

To Begin: Cut out playing cards, fold on dotted lines and tape ends together. Place cards in envelope. Cut out die, fold and tape. Cut out playing pieces.

To Play: Each player selects a playing piece and places it on "Start." Each player rolls the die. The person who rolls the lowest number moves first. Players take turns rolling the die and following instructions on each square to advance. When a player lands on a question square, he must draw a question from the envelope. He must answer the question within three tries before advancing to the next square.

To Win: The winner is the first person to reach Safety. To land on Safety, the player must roll the exact number.

Note: Students may make and use their black history question cards. Students may also use a plastic die.

- Answer two questions to advance
- Answer one question to advance
- Roll the number of letters in your first name to advance
- Answer two questions to advance
- Free Space — Advance one space
- Answer two questions to advance
- Answer one question to advance
- Answer three questions to advance
- Roll a one and answer one question to advance
- Safety
- Answer two questions to advance
- Start — Answer one question to advance
- Answer two questions to advance
- Roll a three to advance
- Answer one question to advance
- Roll a four within three tries to advance

GA1345

Playing Pieces

Cut out playing pieces.

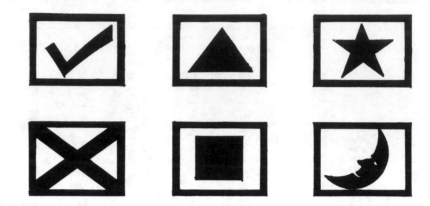

Paper Die

Cut out figure, fold on lines and tape sides together.

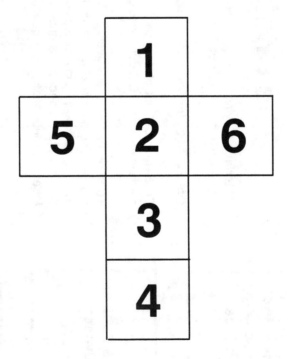

GA1345

Playing Cards

Strict laws that regulated the life of a slave	Black Codes
A slave was owned by a _____.	master, mistress or slave owner
In the South slaves worked in _____, _____ and _____.	cotton, rice, tobacco fields
A sale where Blacks were sold into slavery	an auction
A machine to process large amounts of cotton	a cotton gin
Slave ownership became a symbol of _____ and _____.	wealth, power
They were considered property by their masters.	slaves
The homeland of many slaves	Africa
A person who agreed to work as a servant for five to seven years	an indentured servant

He wrote a book called *Twelve Years a Slave*.	Solomon Northrup
By 1790 there were over 56,000 of these in the Colonial United States.	free Blacks
They founded the Free African Society in Philadelphia.	Richard Allen and Absolom Jones
A dried vegetable shaped like a dipper was called a _____.	drinking gourd
If a free Black was caught without this, he could be sold as a slave.	special certificate
It was a crime to teach free Blacks to _____ and _____.	read, write
A Black who slipped away from a plantation was called a _____.	runaway or fugitive
Name ways that a slave might become free.	born free, freed by his master, bought his freedom, ran to freedom
Songs sung by slaves to help them bear the burden of hard work	spirituals

GA1345

"O' freedom! O' freedom! O' freedom over me!" are words from a _____.	slave song
Plans by groups of slaves to escape were called _____.	slave revolts or uprisings
He planned the largest slave revolt in the history of the United States.	Denmark Vessey
One of the best-known slave revolts that took place in Southampton County, Virginia, was planned by _____.	Nat Turner
Between 1750 and 1850 more than _____ slave revolts took place.	400
In 1800 he planned a daring slave revolt in Henrico County, Virginia.	Gabriel Prosser
The drinking gourd represented this group of stars.	The Big Dipper
Slaves used this star to find their way to the North.	North Star
Large cotton, tobacco or sugarcane farms were called _____.	plantations

GA1345

The Revolutionary Era

In the early years, the thirteen American Colonies were being ruled by Great Britain. After the French and Indian War (1754-1761), King George of Great Britain imposed taxes on the colonies to help pay for the cost of the war. He called for a new system of governing the colonies. Stricter rules were passed to enforce the tax laws. The colonists resisted these new laws and taxes. They felt that they should rule themselves. When the British rules were protested by the colonies, British soldiers called Red Coats were sent to enforce the rules. On March 5, 1770, a mob of colonials threatened to attack a British guard. Leading the mob was a tall black man named Crispus Attucks. When the order to fire was given, Crispus Attucks was the first to be killed by the British gunfire. Two other colonials died instantly. One died shortly and the fifth several days later. These five were the first to lose their lives in what was called the Boston Massacre, the beginning of the Revolutionary War. When the Revolutionary War began, some 5000 were Blacks among the 300,000 soldiers who fought for independence. Black Americans fought in every major battle of the American Revolution. Even though they were not free themselves, they fought gallantly for the thirteen colonies to be free of British rule.

These first brave soldiers who died in the Revolutionary War were buried together. A monument with their names stands on the Boston Common in Boston, Massachusetts.

On March 25, 1988, legislation was passed to build a memorial to the brave Black American soldiers who fought against the British in the Revolutionary War. The memorial will be placed in the main tourist district in Washington, D.C.

In Memory Of

When a brave soldier is killed at war, he/she is usually remembered in some way. Sometimes a person is remembered in a memory poem. A memory poem tells something about the person who is to be remembered. When the memory poem is placed on a tombstone it is called an epitaph.

Example: A memory poem about an inventor
Here lies a man that was great
Who did not wait.
He used his knowledge
Before it was too late.

Write a memory poem on the tombstone below honoring Crispus Attucks, the black American who was the first to die in the Revolutionary War.

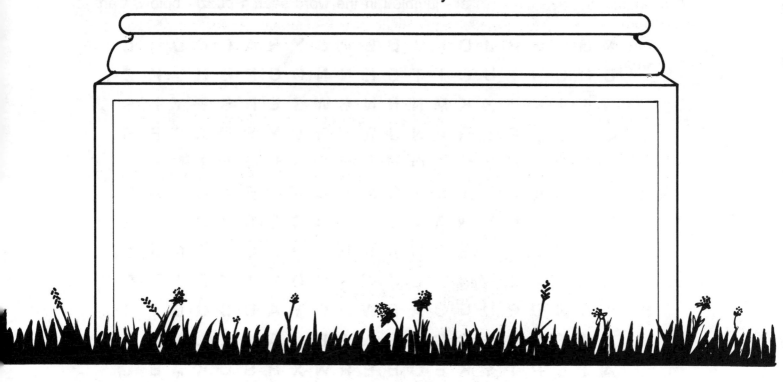

Below list other ways in which a person might be remembered.

Example: 1. A book might be donated to a library in the person's name.

2. _____
3. _____
4. _____
5. _____
6. _____
7. _____
8 _____
9 _____
10. _____

The Original Thirteen

Between 1607 and 1733 thirteen permanent colonies were set up along the Atlantic Coast of North America. The colonies were governed by Great Britain. They were the beginning states that made up our present United States.

Many Americans lived in the original thirteen colonies. Most were slaves. The 1790 census showed that Americans made up twenty percent of the colonial population. In South Carolina, Black Americans outnumbered Whites seven to one. In Georgia one out of every three Americans was black. In Maryland three out of ten Americans were black, and in Delaware one out of every five Americans was black. Black Americans also made up a good portion of the population in other colonies as well. One out of every six Americans in North Carolina was black; one out of every seven Americans in New York was black and one out of every eight Americans in Rhode Island was black. The original thirteen colonies are jumbled in the word search puzzle below. Can you find them?

```
N B J G B J D L J B E P S Y H A C C D U L
D H C R T U C I T C E N N O C P B H Y K Z
Q O I V M X K M N N N E W J E R S E Y L S
Q V V H P J R A N J R W R V Y F K A S F B
E I R B U D O S O U T H C A R O L I N A I
W Q H K G L Y S R Q M A O W W B F G S N C
D C V E C L W A T T A M D D Q A X R Z I W
S H V C V T E C H W P P E U E O L O Q J F
E Z Z A I W N H C Z W S G D V I N E T Y O
G U N D R U H U A E W H Q Y A D S G D I O
J I F V G F G S R D A I B J A J L L N M Z
A T E P I Y K E O B E R W X H S C K A B L
V O F H N R W T L R E E E L B I G E L N K
D C H T I Z T T I U Y C Q B V R Y K Y L D
A O K I A B N S N U F Y D C T Z B J R P E
X Y Q Q Z H A H A K B O T H W Q M R A N F
S U X G F N L P E X O L W B Z H G A M T R
```

Can you find these words?

South Carolina	Maryland	New Hampshire	Massachusetts
Pennsylvania	New York	New Jersey	Rhode Island
Connecticut	North Carolina	Virginia	Delaware

GA1345

Where in the USA?

Locate each of the thirteen original colonies on the map. The names of the colonies are listed below. Use the ZIP code abbreviation for each state.

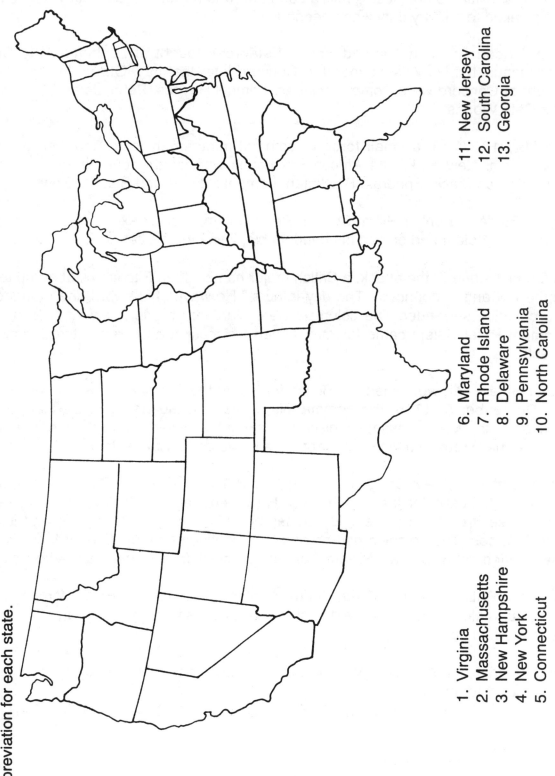

1. Virginia
2. Massachusetts
3. New Hampshire
4. New York
5. Connecticut

6. Maryland
7. Rhode Island
8. Delaware
9. Pennsylvania
10. North Carolina

11. New Jersey
12. South Carolina
13. Georgia

GA1345

On the Battlefield

On April 19, 1775, the first day of the American Revolution, African Americans served in all of the militia companies. A militia company was a group of citizens who stood ready to be called to military duty when needed.

One African American named Prince Estabrook fought at Lexington and Concord, Massachusetts. He was wounded at Concord later that day. Other black soldiers who fought at Concord were Pomp Blackman, Lemuel Haynes, Peter Salem, Cuff Whitmore and Cato Woods.

On May 10, 1775, a small force of colonial minutemen took Ticonderoga on Lake Champlain, New York. The African Americans who fought courageously in this battle were Primas Black, Epheram Blackman, Lemuel Haynes and Barzillai Lew.

In the Battle of Bunker Hill at Boston, Peter Salem, a black ex-slave, became the hero of the day. Salem had gained his freedom by joining the militia.

In the last stage of the attack, a British major named John Pitcairn climbed up to the top of the fort and announced, "The day is ours." He waved his sword and demanded that the colonies surrender. The colonials were startled; no one knew what to do. At that moment Peter Salem came forward, aimed his musket and fired hitting Pitcairn in the chest.

Peter Salem had weakened the British forces and temporarily saved the colonial army. On December 5, 1775, the commanding officer at the Battle of Bunker Hill sent a petition to the Massachusetts legislature asking that Salem Poor, another black hero of the war, be "properly rewarded" for being a brave and gallant soldier.

At the Battle of Great Bridge in Virginia, the British leader Lord Dunmore had recruited African Americans for the British army. He urged black slaves to fight with the British and be set free from slavery. By December 1775 nearly 300 slaves had joined the British forces. The colonies had organized a continental army. One of those serving in the Continental Army was William Flora, a free black from Portsmouth, Virginia.

During a British attack at Great Bridge, William Flora held off British forces and stood his ground alone. Flora was held in high honor by his fellow soldiers and his officers for such a brave act.

At that Battle of Yorktown, Virginia, James Robinson, a Maryland slave was given a gold medal for bravery.

GA1345

Battle Sheet

Listed below are the names of twelve black soldiers who fought during the Revolutionary War. Complete the chart by giving the battle in which each fought and the place of the battle.

Name of Soldier	Battle or Conflict	Battle Site (place)
1. Prince Estabrook		
2. Pomp Blackman		
3. Primas Black		
4. Lemuel Haynes		
5. Epheram Blackman		
6. William Flora		
7. Peter Salem		
8. Barzillai Lew		
9. Cuff Whitmore		
10. Salem Poor		
11. James Robinson		
12. Cato Woods		

GA1345

Great Black Patriots of the Revolutionary War

Black soldiers of the Revolutionary War showed great courage as they fought bravely for the love of the country that continued to deny them their freedom.

Prince Whipple was a wealthy African lad who was sent to America at the age of ten to get an education. Instead, he was captured and sold into slavery by a sea captain at Baltimore, Maryland. He earned his freedom by serving in the Revolutionary War. He was one of the soldiers who crossed the Delaware River with George Washington.

Barzillai Lew was born in Groton, Massachusetts, in 1743 to free parents. He first fought in the French and Indian War, then as a soldier in the Continental Army. He performed dangerous and daring guerrilla warfare against the British "Red Coats."

Seymour Burr was born a slave in the state of Connecticut. He tried to join the British Army to fight for his freedom. The British had promised freedom to all slaves who would join their army and fight for them. Seymour was captured when he attempted to join the British. He later joined the Continental Army as a soldier. He fought at Bunker Hill with the 7th Massachusetts regiment. He was granted his freedom after the war and settled in Canton, Massachusetts.

Lemuel Haynes was born in 1753. He had a white mother and a black father. When he was young, his mother deserted him. He was reared by a deacon in the Congregational Church. Lemuel later became a minister. His training for the ministry was interrupted when the Revolutionary War began. He became a soldier in the Continental Army. After the war, he completed his training for the ministry and became a licensed preacher in the Congregational Church.

Saul Matthews was a soldier and spy for the Continental Army. He was born a slave in Virginia but earned his freedom after serving in the Revolutionary War. Once during the war he penetrated the British lines and gathered important information for the Continental Army. Because of his daring deed, Matthew was granted his freedom by the Virginia legislature.

Joseph Ranger was a seaman in the Virginia Navy during the Revolutionary War. He was a free man from Virginia. He rendered many years of service to the Navy. He later served on four of Virginia's warships. After his discharge in 1787 he was paid a pension of $96 a year and a 100-acre tract for his services to the Navy.

Samuel Charlton was a slave, but when his master died he was set free. He became a soldier in the Continental Army at the age of sixteen. He was sent to the war to substitute for his master. Charlton fought in battles at Brandywine, Germantown and Monmouth. The battle of Monmouth on June 28, 1778, was the last major battle in the north.

28

GA1345

Edward Hector showed great courage as a soldier in the Battle of Brandywine Creek in 1777. Once when General George Washington's soldiers had to retreat, Hector was in charge of the ammunition wagon when he was ordered to abandon the wagon and retreat. Hector did not retreat. Instead he picked up the muskets (guns) that had been left by fleeing soldiers and retired safely with the ammunition wagons. He performed such a courageous act that attempts were made for him to receive a pension. But it wasn't until 1833, one year before his death, that the Pennsylvania legislature voted him a pension of $40 for his services during the war.

Oliver Cromwell was a brave soldier in the Revolutionary War. He was one of the soldiers who crossed the Delaware River on Christmas night in 1776 in a surprise attack on the British troops. At the age of one hundred, he found great pleasure in telling his wartime adventures. He served in the war longer than most other soldiers. After his discharge from the army he received a pension of $96 a year in recognition for his outstanding military service.

James Armstead was a slave from New Kent County, Virginia. While serving in the Continental Army he carried out a dangerous spy mission. He collected valuable information concerning the British forces. After the war in 1786, the Virginia legislature granted him his freedom. In 1816 he bought forty acres of land. Three years later he was granted a pension of $40 and an award of $100 by the Virginia legislature.

Caesar Tarrant was a slave who served as a seaman in the Revolutionary War. He piloted the ship, the *Patriot,* under the command of Commodore Taylor. During a battle at the Cape of Virginia, he steered the ship with great skill. On November 14, 1786, the Virginia legislature granted him his freedom. Tarrant accumulated a large estate and became an influential member of his community. In 1830 Virginia made a large land grant to his heirs.

Salem Poor was a distinguished soldier in the Battle of Charlestown during the Revolutionary War. In this battle he earned the praise of his officers as a brave and gallant soldier.

Peter Salem was a veteran soldier of the battles of Lexington, Concord and Bunker Hill. He was an ex-slave who had been granted his freedom to serve in the Revolutionary War. In the Battle of Bunker Hill, he fired the shot that killed British Commander Major John Pitcairn. This gave the Continental Army many advantages.

James Robinson was awarded a gold medal for military valor as a soldier in the Battle of Yorktown. He also served in the War of 1812 when he helped General Andrew Jackson defend the city of New Orleans against the British. After the Civil War when he became free, he lived in Detroit until his death at 115 years of age.

William Flora was a valiant soldier of the Revolutionary War. He fought bravely at the Battle of Great Bridge when he held off the British forces and stood his ground alone.

Tack Sisson was an American soldier who showed great bravery when he participated in a raid and helped to capture the commander of the British troops at Newport, Rhode Island.

GA1345

Seaman, Soldier or Spy

Place the correct letter beside the name of each black patriot. Se = Seaman; Sp = Spy; So = Soldier

Use the clues below to fill in the blanks and use the circled letters to reveal the name of the first Black American to die during the Revolutionary War.

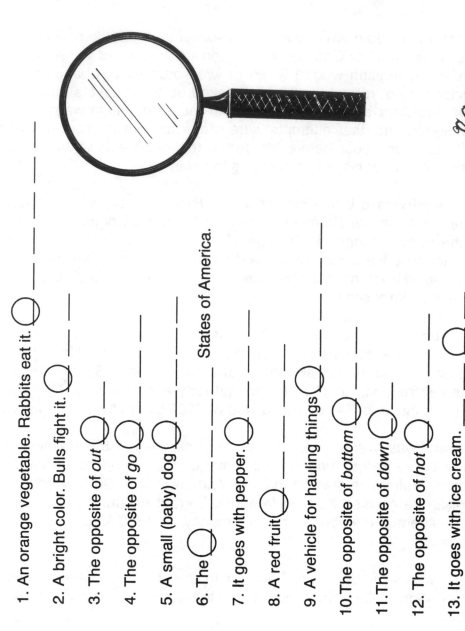

1. Joseph Armstead _____

2. Seymour Burr _____

3. Samuel Charlton _____

4. Oliver Cromwell _____

5. William Flora _____

6. Lemuel Haynes _____

7. Edward Hector _____

8. Barzillai Lew _____

9. Saul Matthews _____

10. Salem Poor _____

11. Joseph Ranger _____

1. An orange vegetable. Rabbits eat it. ⃝ _ _ _ _

2. A bright color. Bulls fight it. _ _ ⃝ _

3. The opposite of *out* _ ⃝ _

4. The opposite of *go* _ ⃝ _ _

5. A small (baby) dog _ ⃝ _ _ _

6. The ⃝ _ _ _ _ _ States of America.

7. It goes with pepper. _ ⃝ _ _

8. A red fruit _ _ ⃝ _ _

9. A vehicle for hauling things _ ⃝ _ _ _

10. The opposite of *bottom* _ ⃝ _

11. The opposite of *down* _ ⃝

12. The opposite of *hot* _ ⃝ _ _

13. It goes with ice cream. _ ⃝ _ _

14. The number after five _ ⃝ _

GA1345

Concentration Game

A game for two to four players

To Begin: Glue the sheet containing the information and name cards to heavy construction paper. Cut each card out. Mix the cards and place each one facedown. Players must make matches between name and information cards.

To Play: Players take turns turning over cards one at a time to make matches. If a player gets a match, he/she keeps the two cards and continues until a mismatch is made. When cards do not match, the player returns both cards facedown and another player begins to play.

To Win: The player with the most matched cards at the end of the game wins.

The game ends when all cards have been matched.

Name Cards

Edward Hector	Samuel Charlton	Caesar Tarrant
Barzillai Lew	Oliver Cromwell	Peter Salem
Crispus Attucks	Joseph Ranger	James Robinson
Seymour Burr	Salem Poor	James Armstead
Prince Whipple	Lemuel Haynes	Saul Matthews

GA1345

Information Cards

First to die in the Boston Massacre	His training to become a minister was interrupted by his service in the Revolutionary War.	First fought in the French and Indian War; performed daring guerilla warfare against British forces.	Showed great courage in the Battle of Brandywine Creek.

Tried first to join British Army; later joined Continental Army	He penetrated the British lines and gathered important spy information.	Served in the Navy during the Revolutionary War. Later served on four of Virginia's warships.	Fought in the Battle of Yorktown Virginia. He was granted a gold medal for bravery.

A wealthy African lad who was sold into slavery; earned his freedom by serving in the Revolutionary Army.	A brave and distinguished soldier in the Battle of Charleston	Crossed the Delaware with General George Washington. Fought at Trenton, Princeton and Brandywine.	He fired the shot that killed the British Commander Major John Pitcairn.

A slave who joined the Continental Army at age 16 as a substitute for his master.	After the Revolutionary War, the Virginia legislature granted him freedom and a pension. He bought forty acres of land.	A seaman during the Revolutionary War, he piloted the *Patriot* with great skill.

GA1345

Search and Supply

Directions

Search for the last name of each of the black Revolutionary War patriots below. Then supply the first names in the blanks.

```
T P S L N W B K J N P C Z F Q U
M J V K X S N E V A M M G W L D
O T Z I C N X Z Z I N R J S Y J
W O F P M U W H E R J L P H S J
K H S F U T T X O B N O M G W S
F B G A O V T T L M O I W W Z R
J L E M K E C H A R L T O N G C
S L O W H E L T C R O M W E L L
M O F R H E T P R O M C S C V H
S E N Y A H Y U P B S S J F Q B
R A N G E R B K T I W Y T R A B
F F L W E I C L S N H B H E I V
O E S E J J H S N S A W R H A H
W K J G M T O W K O M R E N L D
G B J F M N H I D N L N R G W C
V N U P X T P L Y V F J Y A M A
A M F J W R L K A P T V W O T C
```

Can you find these words?

1. _____ Cromwell

2. _____ Charlton

3. _____ Attucks

4. _____ Sisson

5. _____ Flora

6. _____ Burr

7. _____ Armstead

8. _____ Robinson

9. _____ Tarrant

10. _____ Hector

11. _____ Salem

12. _____ Lew

13. _____ Matthews

14. _____ Whipple

15. _____ Haynes

16. _____ Ranger

17. _____ Poor

34

The Declaration of Independence

July 4th is a holiday in the United States celebrated with parades, ball games, picnics and vacations. On July 4, 1776, the United States declared itself free from British rule. A meeting of delegates from the colonies met as the Second Continental Congress to draw up and adopt the document known as the Declaration of Independence. The date of July 4 has been celebrated ever since as the birth of the United States. The Declaration of Independence has been ranked as one of the greatest documents ever produced by man. It tells of the reasons why the colonies wanted freedom from British rule. It also stated that all people have certain rights including the right to say how they will be governed. On July 2, the Congress debated a rough draft of the Declaration written by Thomas Jefferson. Some passages were removed from the original document. The part that condemned King George of Great Britain for encouraging slave trade was deleted.

The original Declaration of Independence is on display in the National Archives Building in Washington, D.C. It is sealed under glass with two other important documents, the Bill of Rights and the United States Constitution.

When the Declaration of Independence was signed and adopted, it freed the colonies; but for thousands of slaves, *freedom* was still a word with little meaning. The second paragraph of the Declaration of Independence states this: "We hold these truths to be self-evident, that all men are created equal, that they are endowed by their Creator with certain unalienable Rights, that among these are Life, Liberty and the pursuit of Happiness."

For many African Americans the Declaration of Independence was a promising step toward equality when it stated that all men are created equal and all have God-given rights, including liberty. Since so many African Americans had fought so courageously during the Revolutionary War, many people argued that they deserted their freedom. They felt that since the war had been fought to gain freedom for all, that the Declaration of Independence should apply to everyone. It has been over two hundred years since the signing of the Declaration of Independence and African Americans continue to struggle for freedom and equality.

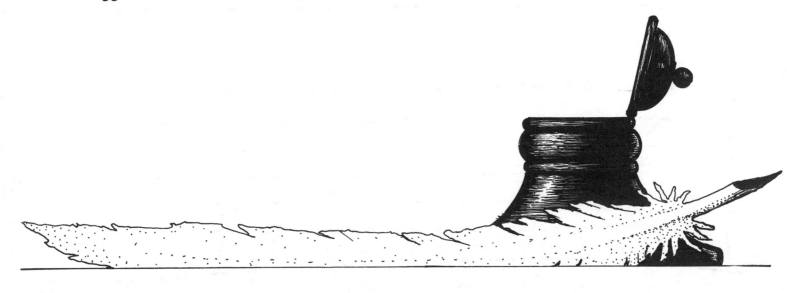

GA1345

My Declaration of Independence

Rewrite the second paragraph of the Declaration of Independence so that it guarantees freedom and equality for African Americans. Be sure to state why they should be granted these rights.

_____
_____
_____
_____
_____
_____
_____
_____
_____
_____
_____
_____
_____
_____
_____
_____
_____
_____
_____

Ask your classmates to sign your Declaration of Independence in the spaces below.

_____ _____ _____ _____
_____ _____ _____ _____
_____ _____ _____ _____

After the Revolutionary War

After the Revolutionary War many leaders began to speak out against slavery. Since many slaves and free Blacks had given their lives and performed many courageous acts during the war, leaders such as Benjamin Franklin, Noah Webster and John Jay spoke out against slavery.

Several states passed legislation and wrote state constitutions to abolish slavery.

Vermont abolished slavery in its constitution of 1777 and Pennsylvania in 1780. Massachusetts and New Hampshire followed in 1783; Rhode Island and Connecticut abolished slavery in 1784. New Jersey began gradually abolishing slavery in 1786 and New York followed in 1799.

None of the southern states ended slavery, but Maryland and North Carolina passed legislation to limit the number of slaves that were imported. In 1787 a law was passed to make sure that slavery would not be permitted in newly explored territory. This law was called the Northwest Ordinance. It was drafted by Thomas Jefferson. A part of the ordinance states that "there shall be neither slavery nor involuntary servitude in the said territory" except for imprisonment for crime. The Northwest Ordinance covered a large area from which the states of Ohio, Indiana, Illinois, Michigan and Wisconsin were created.

GA1345

Show Me

1. Use magic markers, colored pencils or crayons to color the states that were covered by the Northwest Ordinance of 1787. Color the entire area green or blue.

2. Write the date that each northern state banned slavery in the outline of that state.

GA1345

Petition

After the Revolutionary War many felt that because Black Americans had fought so courageously for their country that all slaves should be granted their freedom and slavery should be abolished. You have been selected to appear before the Continental Congress to petition for the abolishment of slavery.

Write your speech in the space below.

_____

_____

_____

_____

_____

_____

_____

_____

_____

_____

_____

_____

_____

_____

_____

_____

_____

_____

_____

_____

GA1345

The U.S. Constitution

After the United States won its independence in the Revolutionary War, it faced great problems. How would it govern itself? How would it collect taxes and enforce laws, stimulate trade and pay its debts? How was it going to deal with Indian tribes and Black Americans?

Two leaders, George Washington and Alexander Hamilton, became more concerned about the problem. On May 14, 1787, a convention of fifty-five delegates was finally called to discuss the problem. They met in Philadelphia, Pennsylvania, to revise the old form of government, the Articles of Confederation, but the delegates did more than revise the Articles of Confederation. They wrote a great plan for governing the United States. It was called the United States Constitution.

The creation of the Constitution was no easy task. Many arguments and disputes had to be settled. One of the conflicts of interest was that of representation. Would the large states send more representatives to the Congress giving them more voting power over the smaller less populated states? After much debate, it was finally decided that one house of Congress would have equal representation regardless of its population and representation according to population in the other house of Congress. This decision was known as the Great Compromise. Another major conflict arose over how slaves would be counted in determining the representation to Congress.

Delegates from the northern states thought that slaves should be counted in determining how much taxes southern states should pay, but they felt that slaves should not be counted to determine representation in Congress. Southern delegates wanted slaves to be counted in deciding how many representatives they could send to Congress but not for taxation. The South had many slaves, and this would give them much voting power in Congress. Naturally the northern states opposed this idea. The Three-fifths Compromise Article 1, Section 2 of the Constitution settled this disagreement. It said that five slaves would be counted as three free persons for both taxation and representation. Another disagreement between the North and South arose over commerce and the slave trade. Delegates from the southern states wanted limited federal power over commerce. They did not want to be taxed for their export crops. They did not want the federal government to stop the slave trade. An agreement called the Commerce Compromise settled this issue. It provided for the Congress to regulate trade by a majority vote.

The Commerce Compromise also stated that Congress could not prohibit slaves to be transported from Africa. It was agreed that foreign slave trade would continue until 1808.

Another part of the Constitution, Article IV, Section 2 (3), stated that a runaway slave who escaped to another state could be returned to his master if the master came to claim him. The Declaration of Independence had offered some hope for the abolishment of slavery, but the original constitution offered very little hope.

GA1345

Name That Issue

Listed below are three major compromises that helped settle disagreements in the writing of the Constitution. Write the issue or problem that each compromise helped to solve.

1. The Great Compromise _____

2. The Three-fifths Compromise _____

3. The Commerce Compromise_____

A Compromise

A compromise is a binding agreement to settle or solve a problem. Suppose that you share a room with a sister or a brother. There are two beds but only one study desk. Your parents expect both of you to use the study desk to work out your assignments. Write a compromise or plan that would provide study time for each of you to use the study desk.

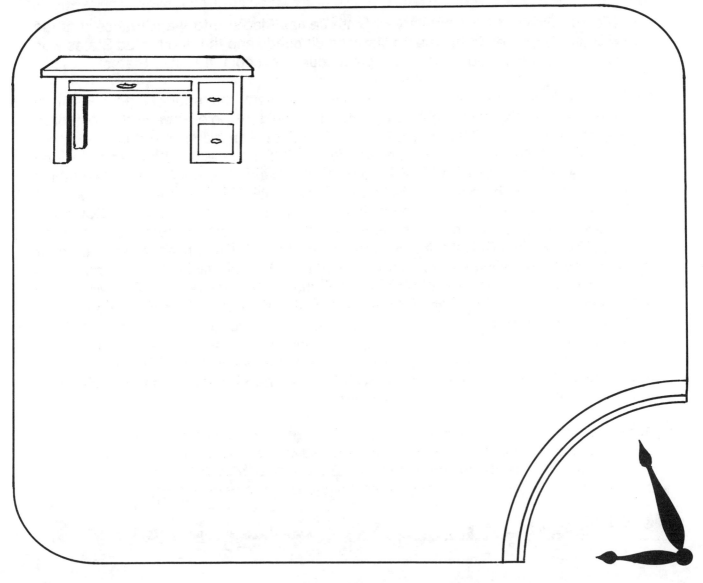

The Louisiana Territory

Did you know that a black man was partially responsible for the acquisition of a large area of the United States called the Louisiana Territory? Here is the story.

In 1801 Thomas Jefferson became president of the United States. He became interested in exploring a land route to the Pacific Ocean. At that time the Mississippi River formed the western boundary of the United States. The territory beyond the Mississippi was known as the Louisiana Territory. It was owned by Spain. Farmers shipped a large variety of goods down the Mississippi River, such as flour, tobacco, pork, bacon, lard, feathers, cider, butter, cheese, apples, potatoes, salt, beeswax, hemp, bear and deer skin. These goods were exchanged for Spanish currency. In a treaty of 1795, Spain had given Americans the right to store and ship goods at the Port City of New Orleans.

In the same month that Jefferson became president, Spain ceded the Louisiana Territory to France. Spain had been a weak nation, but France was a much stronger nation. Jefferson was afraid that France would become aggressive, take over the port city and Americans could not store and ship their goods.

So Jefferson directed his Secretary of State James Madison to warn France that the United States expected to have an outlet for their goods and that the United States was against the transfer of Louisiana to any other country except the United States.

In 1802 Napoleon, the French ruler, had planned to send troops to take possession of Louisiana just as President Jefferson thought he would. Napoleon wanted to establish an empire in America. This caused fear in the Jefferson administration. President Jefferson urged Congress to appropriate money to buy the entire Louisiana Territory and sent negotiators. At this time France also ruled a small country in the West Indies called Haiti. Most of the people of Haiti are descendants of Africans who were brought to Haiti as slaves. In 1791 a slave uprising took place in Haiti. Toussaint L'Ouverture was the leader. L'Ouverture was a black revolutionist. He organized a black army to fight against France. In 1793 the National Convention in France announced freedom for all slaves. In 1799 Toussaint L'Ouverture became ruler of the island of Haiti and set up an independent nation where Blacks would rule themselves. Toussaint ruled wisely and well. Under his leadership Haiti became a very prosperous independent country. In 1802 Napoleon planned to pull Haiti back under the control of France. He decided to subdue Haiti and reestablish slavery. Toussaint was determined that he and his people would never be slaves again. Toussaint resisted Napoleon and his troops, but the Haitian Army under Toussaint fought bravely. They all but wiped out Napoleon's troops. Napoleon's efforts to suppress the revolt had failed.

42

In the meantime, Napoleon had been warned that the United States was considering sending 50,000 troops to take New Orleans. Napoleon knew that his troops had been nearly wiped out in Haiti. On April 30, 1803, France sold the Louisiana Territory to the United States for about $15 million. This vast area of land stretched from the Canadian border south to the Gulf of Mexico. It occupied the large area from the Mississippi River west to the Rocky Mountains. The Louisiana Territory gave the United States great resources.

All or parts of fifteen present day states were carved out of this large territory. They include Louisiana, Arkansas, Missouri, Iowa, Minnesota, North Dakota, South Dakota, Nebraska, Kansas, Oklahoma, Colorado, Wyoming, Montana, Texas and New Mexico.

GA1345

Map Time

On the U.S. map outline below label the states that were carved out of the Louisiana Territory.

44

The Abolition Era

The Abolition Era began as early as 1785. During this era many people who had heard of the harsh treatment of slaves began to speak out against slavery. Both Black and White Americans sometimes worked together to help end slavery. Persons who were against slavery formed antislavery societies. These persons were called abolitionists. Abolitionists believed that slavery was wrong. They believed that all persons living in the United States should have freedom and equal rights. The Quakers and Mennonites were the first religious groups to speak out against slavery. They formed one of the first antislavery societies. Many White Americans became abolitionists and spoke out against slavery.

William Lloyd Garrison, a white abolitionist from Newburyport, Massachusetts, published the first abolitionist newspaper in 1831. It was called *The Liberator.* Other white abolitionists joined Garrison in his stand against slavery. Wendell Phillips and Theodore Parker believed that slavery could be abolished by appealing to people, telling them that slavery was wrong. Two other white abolitionists, James Birney and Theodore Wells, disagreed with Phillips and Parker. They believed that slavery could be abolished by electing politicians who opposed slavery so that they could pass laws to get rid of slavery. They formed the Liberty party and supported James Birney for president of the United States in 1840 and again in 1844, but they were not successful.

John Brown, a white abolitionist from Torrington, Connecticut, believed that guerrilla warfare was the best way to end slavery. On October 15, 1859, he took a small army of seventeen Whites and five black men to capture the federal arsenal at Harpers Ferry, Virginia (now West Virginia). The Arsenal was a government factory where weapons were made and stored. They captured the arsenal and passed out guns and ammunition to slaves in the surrounding area. The slaves were told to use the weapons in a surprise attack on their masters. The news of the arsenal capture spread quickly. When government officials received the news, the United States Marines under the leadership of Robert E. Lee were sent to investigate. Ten of Brown's men including two of his own sons were captured and killed. John Brown escaped at first but was later captured. He was charged with murder, conspiracy and treason against the state of Virginia. On December 2, 1859, John Brown was hanged. John Brown's death caused other abolitionists to work even harder to have slavery abolished. The abolitionists began singing "John Brown's body lies amould'ring in the grave, His soul goes marching on." The abolitionists felt that even though John Brown was dead, this would not stop them. They would continue their fight to abolish slavery. Only eighteen months after John Brown's death, Union soldiers marched into the Civil War singing his praises. To them he had been a brave man who was willing to die for what he believed.

Some White Americans found other ways to help African Americans. Gerritt Smith, a wealthy landowner, gave 120,000 acres of land in the Adirondack Mountains for black settlers. The land was never used because the long hard winters made it impossible for a permanent settlement there.

In 1852 Harriet Beecher Stowe wrote a book called *Uncle Tom's Cabin*. Her book told of the living conditions and harsh treatment of slaves. It was translated into thirty-six languages. People all over the world were shocked when they read of the cruel and inhumane treatment of American slaves. Her book made many people change their minds about slavery.

GA1345

Such famous literary writers as Ralph Waldo Emerson, Henry David Thoreau, Henry Wadsworth Longfellow and John Greenleaf Whittier all supported the abolition movement.

In the mid 1830's two sisters became abolitionists and pioneers in the women's rights movement. Sarah and Angelina Grimke believed that African Americans and women should have the same rights as other people in the United States. Sarah and Angelina Grimke were born to wealthy southern parents in Charleston, South Carolina. Even though they were born and grew up in the South where almost no one spoke out against slavery, they had the courage to stand up for what they believed to be the right thing. They wrote pamphlets and traveled throughout the northeastern United States speaking out against slavery.

In 1837 Elijah Lovejoy, a white newspaper writer, was shot to death and his printing press was thrown in the river in Alton, Illinois, because he printed antislavery articles in his newspaper.

Other white abolitionists included Anthony Benezet, Prudence Crandall, Thaddeus Stevens, Charles Sumner, John Woolman, Lydia Marie Childs, Arthur and Lewis Tappan, Albion Tourgee, George Washington Cable, Levi Coffin and Joel Spingarn.

GA1345

We Believe

A belief is a reason to act or speak out against something. Many Americans believed slavery should be abolished, but they had different opinions as to how it should be abolished.

Complete the chart below by writing in the beliefs of each group or individual.

Groups/Individuals	Beliefs
1. Abolitionists	
2. Wendell Phillips and Theodore Parker	
3 James Birney and Theodore Wells	
4. John Brown	
5. Sarah and Angelina Grimke	

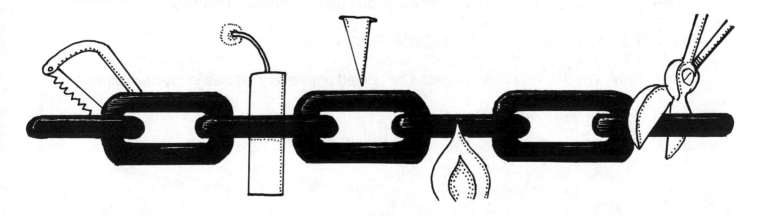

47

GA1345

Chain of Events

Listed below are five major events in the Abolition Era. Arrange the events in chronological order along the chain of events.

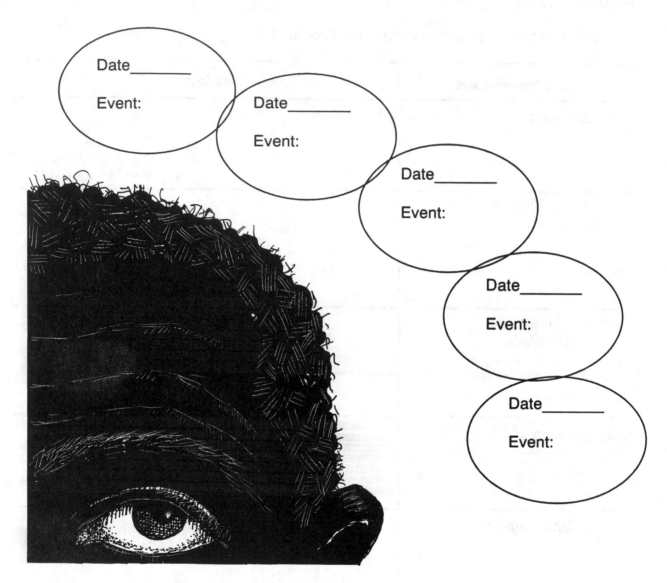

Date_____

Event:

Date_____

Event:

Date_____

Event:

Date_____

Event:

Date_____

Event:

1831: Garrison published the first abolition newspaper.

1859: John Brown used guerrilla warfare in an attempt to abolish slavery.

1852: Harriet Beecher Stowe wrote *Uncle Tom's Cabin.*

1837: Elijah Lovejoy was killed because he printed antislavery articles in his newspaper.

1785: The beginning of the Abolition Era

GA1345

Going Further

Many well-known leaders spoke out against slavery. Some of them are listed below. Use encyclopedias or other reference books and write two or more identification sentences about each person.

1. Benjamin Franklin

_____

_____

2. Noah Webster

_____

_____

3. John Jay

_____

_____

4. Ralph Waldo Emerson

_____

_____

5. Henry David Thoreau

_____

_____

6. John Greenleaf Whittier

_____

_____

7. Henry Wadsworth Longfellow

_____

_____

8. Thaddeus Stevens

_____

_____

9. Charles Sumner

_____

_____

10. Joel Spingarn

_____

_____

GA1345

Famous Black Abolitionists

Black abolitionists led the way in the fight to end slavery. Many worked through antislavery societies and some worked alone. They wrote pamphlets, books and edited newspapers. Others traveled throughout the country speaking out against slavery. Many worked on the underground railroad helping slaves to escape to freedom. This was a very dangerous thing to do. Many black abolitionists were often beaten and harassed by slave owners. The slave owners feared that the abolitionists would cause their slaves to rise up against them.

Early great black abolitionist leaders such as David Walker, Harriet Tubman and Sojourner Truth were willing to give their lives that others might have freedom from slavery.

The abolition movement produced many other black leaders.

Henry Highland Garnet (1815-1882) was born a slave in the state of Maryland. When he was nine years old he and his parents escaped to Pennsylvania. By the age of twenty-two, he had become an outstanding speaker. Garnet later became a minister and served as pastor of the Fifteenth Street Presbyterian Church in Washington, D.C., from 1864-1866. During this time he was invited to preach to the House of Representatives. At the time of his death he was serving as official Minister to Liberia.

Charles Lenox Remond (1810-1873) was born of free parents in the state of Massachusetts. He was a well-educated man. While serving as the offical speaker of the Massachusetts Antislavery Society, Remond traveled throughout New England. In many places where he spoke, people declared him to be the greatest speaker of all times until the great orator Frederick Douglass came along.

Samuel Cornish (1790-1859) was a talented journalist. He was born free in the state of Delaware. He later moved to Philadelphia where he attended school. In 1822 he organized the first black Presbyterian Church. In 1887 he and another great abolitionist, John Russwurm, started the first black newspaper. It was called *Freedom's Journal*. Other black abolitionist leaders such as James McCune Smith, Alexander Crummell, Martin Delany and David Ruggles wrote articles for his newspaper.

Robert Purvis (1810-1898) was born in South Carolina. His father was a wealthy white man and his mother was a mulatto (mixed black and white). Robert Purvis inherited his father's wealth. Even though he appeared white, he thought of himself as being black. He was educated at Amherst College in Massachusetts and then settled in Pennsylvania. He worked to organize the American Anti-Slavery and the Pennsylvania Anti-Slavery Societies. He devoted most of his time, talent and money to the underground railroad. From records that he kept from 1831-1861, he estimated that he sent one slave every day. This comes to a total of 9000 slaves that he helped to freedom in the North.

GA1345

William Still (1821-1902) was the eighteenth child born to a slave mother and an ex-slave father. When he grew up, he devoted much of his time to helping slaves escape on the underground railroad. He later wrote a book called *The Underground Railroad*. It told the story of how he helped 649 slaves escape to freedom. One day while working on the underground railroad, something very interesting happened as he talked with an escaped slave. He discovered that the escaped slave was his own younger brother who had been sold into slavery when he was young.

William Whipple (1805-1885) was the child of a black house servant and her white master. He was reared in his father's household. He developed a theory of nonviolence. He published several pamphlets and articles on the evils of slavery. When his father died, he inherited a successful lumber business. He used a portion of his wealth to help escaping slaves on the underground railroad.

James W.C. Pennington (1809-1870) was born a slave in Washington County, Maryland. When he grew up he trained to be a blacksmith and a brick mason. He could shoe horses and build houses and other structures. When he was older, he ran away from a cruel master to New York. There he acquired his education and became a minister and an outstanding speaker. He was such a great speaker that he was invited to speak before dignitaries in Paris, Brussels and London. In 1849 he wrote a book called *The Fugitive Blacksmith*. It told of his life as a slave and how he escaped to freedom in the North.

James Forten (1766-1842) was born free in Philadelphia. When he was fourteen years old, he joined the navy and served in the Revolutionary War. While serving in the navy, he developed a device to handle ship sails. He became a businessman who owned a sail loft. He employed both Blacks and Whites. With his business he became the wealthiest black man in Philadelphia.

Theodore S. Wright (1797-1847) was born to free parents in Providence, Rhode Island. He became an outstanding minister of the Presbyterian Church. He served in antislavery organizations and was a conductor on the underground railroad in New York.

James McCune Smith (1813-1865) was a highly trained physician. He was born to free parents in New York. He received his education and medical degrees from the University of Glasgow in Scotland. He returned to New York and became a successful medical doctor. He bought two drugstores in New York City. Dr. Smith was an outstanding writer and speaker.

Many other great black leaders gave their time, talent and wealth to the abolition movement.

GA1345

Name That Man

Supply the correct information.

1. He was a highly trained physician. _____

2. He was invited to preach to the House of Representatives. _____

3. He was considered the greatest abolitionist speaker until Frederick Douglass.

   _____

4. He started the first black newspaper._____

5. He worked to organize two antislavery societies. _____

6. He developed a device to handle sails and became a wealthy businessman.

   _____

7. He wrote a book called *The Underground Railroad*. _____

8. He became an outstanding minister in the Presbyterian Church. _____

   _____

9. He developed a theory of nonviolence. _____

10. He wrote a book called *The Fugitive Blacksmith*. _____

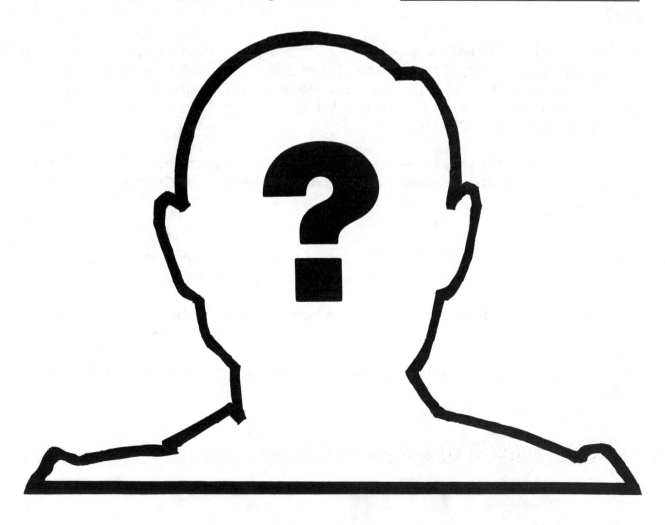

Math-Age-Matics

Calculate the ages of each of these abolitionists at the time of his death.

1. Henry Highland Garnet (1815-1882)

2. Charles Lenox Remond (1810-1873)

3. Samuel Cornish (1790-1859)

4. Robert Purvis (1810-1898)

5. William Still (1821-1902)

6. William Whipple (1805-1885)

7. James W.C. Pennington (1809-1870)

8. James Forten (1766-1842)

9. Theodore S. Wright (1797-1847)

10. James McCune Smith (1813-1865)

11. Which abolitionist was the oldest at his death? _____

12. Which abolitionist was the youngest at his death? _____

Arrange the names of the abolitionists on the time line below according to their ages.

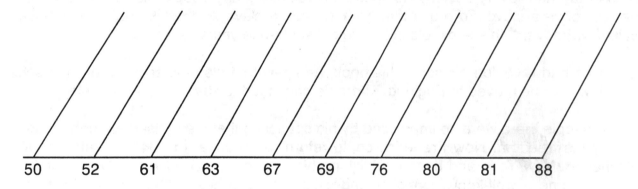

| 50 | 52 | 61 | 63 | 67 | 69 | 76 | 80 | 81 | 88 |

GA1345

Frederick Douglass

In 1841 a tall, dark, handsome man was asked to speak to a group of people who had gathered to discuss ways of abolishing slavery. The man was Frederick Douglass and the people were members of the Massachusetts Antislavery Society.

Frederick Douglass spoke so well that he gained everyone's attention. He was later chosen by the society to travel throughout the country to speak out against slavery. Frederick Douglass was the best person for the job because he was a good speaker, and he had been a slave. He was born a slave in Talbot County, Maryland, in 1817. He was the son of a white father and a black slave mother. As a child, he was eager to learn to read and write, but teaching a slave to read and write was against the law. So Frederick learned secretly from his white playmates and taught himself to read and write. When he grew up, he longed to be free. He noticed that slaves who fought back when they were beaten, were not beaten as much as those who did not fight back. So when Frederick was beaten, he began to fight back. When he was sixteen years old, he gave his master so much trouble that he was sent to a "slave breaker." A slave breaker would whip and beat a slave until he agreed not to give his master any more trouble. Still, Frederick fought back. The slave breaker could not break Frederick. When he was nineteen years old, Frederick became dissatisfied with his life as a slave. He began making plans to escape to the North. At the age of twenty-one, he borrowed the identification papers of a free black man and escaped by train and ferry from Baltimore to New York. His original name was Frederick Augustus Washington Bailey, but he changed his name to Frederick Douglass when he escaped. He finally settled in Bedford, Massachusetts, and began working in a shipyard. It was there that he addressed the members of the antislavery society. He spoke so well that many people did not believe that he was once a slave. To prove that he had been a slave, Frederick published a book called *Narratives*. This book told of his life of twenty-one years as a slave.

Since he had revealed himself in his book, he knew that his master could easily track him down, so he moved to England. There he continued to speak out against slavery.

Some people there were so impressed by his speeches that they raised enough money to buy his freedom. Now Frederick could return to America. In 1847 he returned to Rochester, New York, and began publishing his newspaper, *The North Star*. Frederick soon became a well-known speaker and writer. He also became known as the most outstanding Black American of his day and time.

Frederick Douglass became a leader in other areas as well. He was once beaten and thrown from a train because he sat in the first-class sections where Blacks were not allowed to sit. Still he continued to fight for freedom and equality for his people. His actions finally paid off, when the New England railroads no longer required Blacks to sit in special places. His actions also helped to eliminate segregation in schools in Rochester, New York.

During the Civil War, Frederick Douglass served as an advisor to President Abraham Lincoln. He called on President Lincoln to abolish slavery and enroll black troops as soldiers in the Union Army. Early in 1863 when Congress approved black enlistment in the Union Army, Frederick Douglass organized two regiments of black soldiers. His own sons fought in the Union Army.

After the war ended in 1865, Frederick Douglass became a leader in business and politics. In 1874 he became president of the Freedman's Saving and Trust Company. In 1877 he became a United States Marshal. In 1880 he was appointed recorder of deeds for Washington, D.C. Nine years later, he became American Consul-General to Haiti. Frederick was interested not only in the rights of Blacks Americans, but he also thought that women should have equal rights too. On February 20, 1895, he attended a women's rights meeting. As he told his wife about the events of the meeting, he was suddenly stricken with a massive heart attack and died. Frederick Douglass had lived for seventy-eight years.

When he was laid to rest in Rochester, New York, he was mourned by thousands of people. Frederick Douglass, the greatest black speaker, writer, historian and abolitionist, had given most of his adult life fighting for freedom and equality for African Americans and women.

If you visit Washington, D.C., you can visit Cedar Hill, Frederick Douglass' home. It was here that Frederick Douglass conducted much of his work. This beautiful Victorian house overlooks the nation's capital. In the Visitors' Center you can see exhibits and audiovisuals on Douglass' life and work. You can also see gifts and other items that he received from such famous persons as Harriet Beecher Stowe, Abraham Lincoln, William Lloyd Garrison and many others.

GA1345

Life Signs

Place an important event from Frederick Douglass' life on each road sign above the correct date.

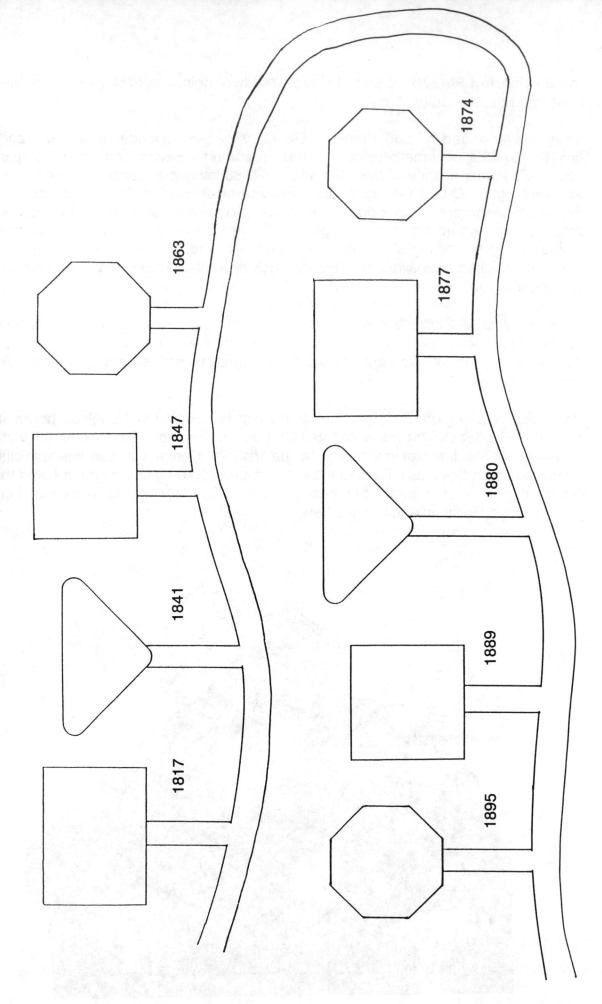

GA1345

The Frederick Douglass Creative Arts Center

On 46th Street in Manhattan, New York, stands the Frederick Douglass Creative Arts Center. This Center is the only such place in the country where Blacks and other minorities can develop their writing skills. At the Center, students can take classes and workshops in writing poetry, creative writing, playwriting, television writing, journalism (newspaper writing) and acting.

The Center sponsors a Black Roots Festival each year to give young writers a chance to meet famous Black American writers and performers. Some of the writers and actors that have attended the festival are James Baldwin, Maya Angelou, Toni Morrison, Quincy Troupe, Amiri Baraka and August Wilson.

The Center is directed by Fred Hudson who is a famous black writer himself. He writes plays and scripts for movies and television shows.

When the Center opened in 1971, it had only eight students. Today the Center has over two hundred students a year. Students come from New York, Connecticut, New Jersey and other states to attend classes at the Center. Many of these students earn awards and recognition for their work on major television networks, in Hollywood studios and Broadway.

The Frederick Douglass Creative Arts Center has won many trophies and recognitions for helping Black Americans and other minority writers and actors. Banks and large corporations donate money to operate the Center. In 1990 the Center celebrated its nineteenth anniversary for helping Blacks and other minorities become better writers and performers.

The Frederick Douglass Creative Arts Center continues to live up to its namesake, Frederick Douglass, the famous black speaker, writer, abolitionist and statesman.

GA1345

Secrets (Part 1)

The underground railroad had its own special language, signals, secret words and secret messages that only the escaping slaves and those who helped them could understand.

The escaping slaves were called *passengers*. Those who sheltered the passengers and gave them food and clothing were called *stationmasters* or *station agents*. Those who led the slaves from one secret hiding place to another were called *conductors*. The secret places such as barns and haylofts, abandoned houses and attics where the slaves stopped for food and clothing were called *stations* or *depots*. Food and clothing were called *fuel.*

There were also hand signals. A *closed fist* meant safety. An *open hand* meant danger.

There were also secret words, a sort of special language. *Forward* meant to send slaves on to the next station. *Travel conditions* meant safety of travel. *Throw a switch* meant to change directions.

The year is 1850. You are living in the North where slavery is illegal. You have decided to become a stationmaster on the underground railroad. As a stationmaster you will hide, feed and clothe runaway slaves and send them on to the next station. Before you can become a stationmaster, you must memorize all of the secret words, signals and secret messages. If you send the wrong signal or give the wrong message, you could cause escaping slaves to be caught and returned to their masters to be dealt with harshly or to be killed.

Memorize each word, its meaning and signal. Study the words with a friend. When you are sure that you have learned the secrets necessary to become a stationmaster, you are ready to complete Part 2 of this activity.

GA1345

Secrets (Part 2)

It is late night, 11:33 to be exact. You hear a distant rap of three successive knocks at the door. You peep through the shutter. By the lamplight you can see a shadow with a raised, closed fist. Without a word, you open the door. It is a messenger. He hands you a note and slips off into the darkness. The note reads:

Dear Friend,
Tomorrow night if *travel conditions* are good, you can expect three *passengers.*
Please give them *fuel* and *forward.* If you have to *throw a switch*, you will be notified.

You have a good *station* for *passengers.*

Rewrite the note and replace the italicized secret words with their meanings.

Secret Code Book

Create a secret code book for an escaping slave. Fold two sheets of paper in half to measure 8 1/2" x 5 1/2" (21.6 x 13.97 cm).

Fold a piece of construction paper in the same way. Slip the folded paper into the construction paper and staple along the spine to make a booklet.

Write hand signals, secret passwords and messages in your secret booklet. Be sure to give the meaning of each.

Use an encyclopedia or other reference books to write a paragraph about three famous agents or conductors on the underground railroad. Make your selection from the name bank below.

Illustrate your booklet with pictures or drawings.

Exchange your booklet with a friend and ask him/her to evaluate it.

Write a title on the front cover of your booklet and decorate the front and back with pictures or drawings with crayons or markers.

Name Bank

William Still	Theodore S. Wright	Josiah Henson
Harriet Tubman	Levi Coffin	David Ruggles
John Brown		

GA1345

A Thousand Miles to Freedom

Running a Thousand Miles to Freedom is the title of an autobiography written by William and Ellen Craft. It tells of their daring escape from a Macon, Georgia, plantation to freedom in the North. One day William Craft decided that he and his wife Ellen were tired of their disgusting lives as slaves. They began a carefully planned scheme to escape to freedom. William, a cabinetmaker saved his small earnings until he had enough money to buy his wife Ellen a man's suit. Their plans would go like this: Ellen, his wife, was a very light-skinned woman. She would dress up as a white man and her darker husband William would pretend to be her slave. She would be going North for medical treatment. She would pretend to be hard of hearing so that no one would ask too many questions. She would wear bandages on her arms so that she would not be asked to sign hotel registers. Ellen could not read or write.

In January of 1849, the Crafts put their plan into action. They boarded a train and headed north to Philadelphia. They traveled first class all the way and stayed at the best hotels without any questions. Both William and Ellen played their parts well. William the slave looked after his "master's" every need. As the train roared through the countryside, William's and Ellen's hearts would pound every time someone would look their way. The punishment for runaway slaves was harsh. If at any time they were recognized, they could be captured and returned to their master. Many runaways were sold "down the river" into Mississippi or Louisiana where slave masters dealt more harshly with their slaves. It was a long trip from Macon, Georgia, to Philadelphia and the added pressure of being found out made the trip seem even longer.

Finally they reached Philadelphia where a conductor on the underground railroad took them to his home. Later they were taken on to Boston, Massachusetts. When the Anti-Slavery Society learned that the Crafts were being sought after as fugitive slaves, they moved them even further–to London, England. It had been a long scary trip, but William and Ellen had made it.

In London, William worked for a London business. After the Civil War, the Crafts returned to their home state of Georgia. They bought a plantation of their own and started a school for black children near Savannah, Georgia.

A Master Plan

You have learned that you will soon be sold "down the river." Tonight as you lie awake, you begin to make plans for you and your family to escape to the North. You have a mother and father, an older brother and a younger sister. Remember, you have many things to think about. Will everyone try to escape at the same time, or will one or two family members go ahead and send back for the others? If so, who will go ahead and who will stay? Will you go by underground railroad or some other great creative plan? Be creative and nonviolent.

Reveal the master plan for your escape in the space below. Use drawings if needed to make your plans as clear as possible.

GA1345

An Ingenious Plan

Henry Brown was a slave in Richmond, Virginia. He devised an ingenious plan for escaping slavery. He had a carpenter friend make a box that was two feet (60.96 cm) wide; three feet (91.44 cm) long and two feet, eight inches (81.28 cm) deep. The box would be shipped to a freight station in Philadelphia via the Adam Express Company.

While there was nothing dangerous about shipping a box, there was grave danger in shipping this one. This was no ordinary box. It contained very precious cargo. You see, Henry Brown had asked his friend to build this box for him. He would be shipped to Philadelphia. On the day of the shipping, Henry Brown waved good-bye to his friends and family, climbed in his box and asked his friends to nail it shut. With him he took a container of water and some biscuits. His friends posted a sign on the box that read *this side up*, and off to the freight station they carried their unsuspecting box. The trip from Richmond to Philadelphia took thirty-six hours.

Once in Philadelphia, the box was delivered to the antislavery office. The office had been notified of Brown's plans, and the officers there waited anxiously for his arrival. As soon as the box arrived, the lid was removed. Henry Brown was alive and well. It is reported that when the box was open, Henry Brown arose, held out his hand for a handshake and said, "How do you do, gentlemen." From that time forward Henry Brown was known as Henry "Box" Brown.

Henry Brown's box contained only biscuits and water. List three other items that you would have included.

1. _____

2. _____

3. _____

If you had to spend twelve hours in a secluded place such as your bedroom, how would you spend your time? Show your activities on the schedule below.

8:00 a.m. _____

9:00 a.m. _____

10:00 a.m. _____

11:00 a.m. _____

12:00 a.m. _____

1:00 p.m. _____

2:00 p.m. _____

3:00 p.m. _____

4:00 p.m. _____

5:00 p.m. _____

6:00 p.m. _____

7:00 p.m. _____

8:00 p.m. _____

GA1345

Brochure

You are a famous artist/illustrator. You have been asked to make a brochure to encourage students to study at the Frederick Douglass Creative Arts Center.

Fold a sheet of 8 1/2" x 11" (21.6 x 27.94 cm) paper in half so that it measures 5 1/2" x 8 1/2" (13.97 x 21.6 cm).

Write an interesting slogan or title on the front of the folded paper and use colored pencils, crayons or markers to illustrate the cover. Now open the paper and write some interesting information about the Center.

Write your ideas in the space below; then use them to make your brochure.

_____

_____

_____

_____

_____

_____

_____

_____

_____

_____

_____

_____

_____

_____

_____

_____

_____

GA1345

Harriet to the Rescue!

One famous abolitionist was Harriet Tubman, the brave conductor of the underground railroad. One day Harriet was in Troy, New York, visiting a cousin. While there she participated in a daring attempt to rescue a fugitive slave. Here is the story.

On April 27, 1859, a runaway slave named Charles Nalles was being returned to his owner. Nalles had been a slave on a plantation in Culpepper County, Virginia, but he had escaped to Pennsylvania. He later moved to Troy, New York, and joined his family that had been freed under the terms of their master's will. Nalles had settled in New York and had become a coachman for an outstanding family there. Nalles could neither read nor write, so he sought the help of a citizen to help him write letters. When the citizen found that Nalles was an escaped slave, he contacted Nalles' owner back in Virginia. Nalles' owner sent a deputy to arrest Nalles and bring him back to Virginia.

On the morning of April 27, 1859, Nalles went to the town's bakery to pick up bread for the family for whom he worked. It was then that he was arrested by a deputy United States Marshal under the Fugitive Slave Law which stated that by law a runaway slave could be caught and returned to his owner. Four hours later Nalles had appeared before the United States Commissioner for a hearing and had been found guilty as a runaway slave and ordered returned to his owner in Virginia.

In the meantime the family for whom Nalles worked became worried when he did not return from the bakery on time. When they went to look for Nalles, they learned that he was being held in custody in the U.S. Commissioner's office. Several people had gathered around the office building protesting that Nalles should not be sent back to slavery in Virginia. The crowd grew larger as more people jammed the street. They could see Nalles as he faced a window from the second floor of the building. The crowd did not want Nalles to be taken back to Virginia. Several people gave donations to help buy Nalles' freedom, but they were turned down. A lawyer was appointed for Nalles. The lawyer made arrangements for Nalles to bring his case to court. The police, a deputy

Harriet Tubman

sheriff and a deputy marshal tried to take Nalles through the crowd of people to the courthouse two blocks away. On the way to the courthouse, the crowd became an angry mob. They snatched Nalles away from the law officials. It was then that the famous Harriet Tubman came to the rescue. According to a witness, Harriet rushed up to Nalles and held onto him. She was beaten repeatedly, but she held on to Nalles, talking to him and encouraging him for more than a half an hour. Harriet held on to Nalles and struggled with the officers until the officers lost their grips and Nalles was torn away from them. The crowd helped Nalles to a waiting rowboat where he was quickly rowed across the Hudson River at Albany County, New York. When he reached the other side of the river he was again arrested and taken to the justice of the peace office. In the meantime Harriet and a crowd of four hundred people had crossed the river by ferryboat. They jammed the building. A large black man kicked in the door where Nalles was being held. He was struck down by the sheriff's hatchet. His body kept the door from closing. Harriet rescued Nalles. A passerby gave his horse and wagon to help Nalles escape. Nalles was driven to Schenectady, New York, and then to Canada. Money was raised to buy Nalles' freedom. In 1860 Nalles returned to Troy, New York, with his family and then later moved to Washington, D.C. The people in his hometown thought of Nalles as a hero. They were proud of the part that they played in helping Nalles to escape to freedom, and he was proud of them for helping him.

Report It

You are a reporter for the *Daily Gazette* newspaper. Prepare a news report of the escape of Charles Nalles. Write your report underneath the news headline on the newspaper below.

Harriet Tubman to the Rescue

GA1345

Colonization

Some African Americans thought that their people would never be treated fairly in America. Some hoped for a better life in Africa. Others wanted to separate themselves from white America in a portion of the United States. Still others wanted a colony to be established in Central or South America. Four black men who dreamed of a life somewhere outside of the United States were Marcus Garvey, Martin Delaney, Henry Mac-Neal and Paul Cuffe.

Martin R. Delaney was a physician who trained at Harvard University. He was born in the state of Virginia in 1812. When the Fugitive Slave Act became law in 1850, Martin worried that America was not the "land of the free and the home of the brave" because many Blacks who escaped slavery could by law be returned to their masters, and free Blacks without proof of their identity could be brought to the South and sold into slavery. Martin turned his attention to the American Colonization Society and thought of ways to find another place for what he called "people of African descent."

In 1859 he attended a Colonization Society meeting in Chatham, Canada. He then decided that it was time to put some of his ideas to work. With this in mind he traveled to Africa where he met with eight African kings. He signed a treaty with them to agree to a colony of African Americans settling in their area. He had dreamed of setting up a colony in Africa. Martin Delaney practiced medicine in Chicago and Canada, but most of his time was spent traveling and speaking out on abolition and colonization.

Marcus Garvey was probably best known for his "Back-to-Africa" movement. Marcus was born in 1887 in Jamaica of the West Indies. At the age of sixteen he worked at a printing plant in Kingston, Jamaica. Marcus was a man of many talents, but he was especially good at speaking and organizing groups of people. At an early age, he became the spokesman for his people of the island. He was educated at London Uni-

Martin R. Delaney

68

versity and traveled throughout Europe and North Africa observing the social conditions of his people. He then returned to Jamaica and organized the Jamaica Improvement Association. Two years later he came to America and organized the University Negro Improvement Association. Through this organization Marcus gained a large number of followers for his "Back-to-Africa" movement. Marcus Garvey had dreamed of establishing a nation of many black families in Africa. These families would rule their own country. He dreamed of Blacks having their own businesses, grocery stores, printing shops, restaurants and motels. His plan for setting up the nation was to spread to groups of African Americans like himself who felt that Blacks would never be treated fairly in the United States. All of Garvey's plans required large sums of money. In 1925 his "Back-to-Africa" movement failed when he was accused of using the mail to collect money for a steamship called the *Black Star Line*. He had planned to use the ship to transport Black Americans back to Africa. Even though Garvey's plans did not work, he had helped them to develop a sense of pride for themselves and their ancestor homeland of Africa. He had given them something to think about.

Henry MacNeal was born free in Abbeville, South Carolina. When he was twelve years old his father died. So Henry had to hire out to work in the cotton fields with the slaves. When he was old enough, he learned the alphabet and taught himself to read. At the age of fifteen he ran away and became a messenger boy for an attorney. He later became an African Methodist minister. During the Civil War, President Lincoln appointed him to be chaplain for a black regiment.

After the Civil War he worked with the Freedom's Bureau. In 1868 he fought for the rights of Blacks to hold public office. During this time he became disgusted with the way that Blacks were being treated. He helped to sponsor an expedition of 206 colonists to Liberia in 1878. He had dreamed of setting up an entire colony of Blacks there. His dream turned into a disaster. In later years, Henry received an honorary degree from the University of Pennsylvania and became chancellor of Morris Brown, a predominately black university in Atlanta, Georgia.

Marcus Garvey

GA1345

Dreams, Dreams, Dreams

Three men had dreams of a better life for Black Americans outside of the United States. Write the correct dream above each bed.

Marcus Garvey   **Henry MacNeal**   **Martin Delaney**

In the space below write about one of your dreams.

70

GA1345

Missing You

Suppose that each colonization idea had worked and all Black Americans were shipped to areas outside of the United States. Listed below are five famous black scientists whose works we would not have had.

Select one name and research it to find out the person's major achievement; then write a letter using the form below.

1. George Washington Carver
2. Benjamin Banneker
3. Norbert Rillieux
4 Elijah McCoy
5. Charles Richard Drew

Dear Mr. _____,

We would miss you because you _____

_____

_____

_____

_____

_____

_____

_____

Thank you.
Sincerely,

_____
(Sign your name here.)

71

Paul Cuffe

In 1793 a large ship pulled into the mouth of the Nanticoke River in Maryland. On the outside it looked like any ordinary ship, but this was no ordinary ship. This large beautiful ship belonged to a black man whose name was Paul Cuffe. Cuffe had come to the eastern Maryland shores to buy corn. As his ship pulled into the harbor, many were amazed that a black man could own such a large ship.

At first he was not allowed to come ashore until he produced papers to show that he was the owner of the ship. What the people didn't know was that Paul Cuffe had spent most of his life at sea. He was born near New Bedford, Massachusetts, in 1759. He was born free, but his father was a former slave who had bought his freedom. His father had married an Indian woman from the Wampanoag tribe. Paul was the youngest of his sons. When Paul was in his early teens, his father died and Paul and his brothers had to work to support their sisters and mother. Paul got a job on a whaling ship. This job took him to many places and helped him learn a great deal about sailing. He learned the charts of the seven seas and the rules of navigation. He first earned enough money to purchase a small boat and used it to buy and sell goods. Soon he began to make some profits.

At the age of twenty-five he married and purchased a larger boat of eighteen tons. It was equipped for codfishing. His profits grew and so did his business. By this time Paul had become a very successful boat builder, sea captain and owner of a fleet of ships. Paul's life was a success; but he thought of all the other Blacks, both slave and free, who were toiling in hard labor. The only way that he could help them, he thought, was to find a place outside of America where they all could be free.

In 1811 he traveled to Sierra Leone, West Africa, and organized the friendly Society of Sierra Leone. In 1815 he spent $4000 to transport Black Americans to Sierra Leone to establish a colony. This was a great sum of money in 1815. He had planned more trips to Africa, but they were cancelled due to his poor health. Not only was Paul Cuffe a successful businessman, he was also active in the affairs of his community. In 1797 he purchased a farm and built a school.

Paul Cuffe, the youngster who had begun his life as a whaler, became a wealthy businessman. At his death in 1817 he had accumulated an estate worth more than $20,000. That was a great sum of money for the year 1817. Over his grave is a brief epitaph that reads:

In Memory of
Captain Paul Cuffe
A self-made man
Patriot, *Navigator*, *Educator*,
Philanthropist, Friend,
a *noble* character

File It!

Write five important facts about Paul Cuffe's life on the file cards below.

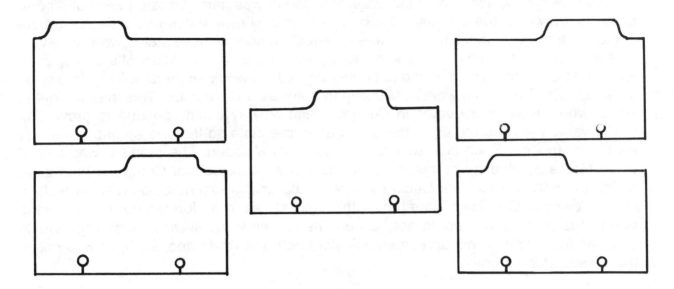

Epitaph

An epitaph is a brief statement that tells something about a person. It is usually placed on the person's tombstone or grave marker.

Design a tombstone for Paul Cuffe and place the epitaph on it. Use a dictionary to find the meaning of each of the italicized words in Paul Cuffe's epitaph. Write the meaning in the space opposite each word.

Patriot_____

_____

Navigator _____

_____

Educator_____

_____

Philanthropist _____

_____

Noble _____

_____

GA1345

The Compromises

The Missouri Compromise

In 1820 the area which is now the state of Missouri was part of a large area of land to the west known as the Louisiana Territory. Soon many new states would be carved out of the large area. At this time there was an equal number of slave states (where slavery was allowed) and free states (where slavery was not allowed). When Missouri applied for admission to the Union, it had to be determined if it would enter as a free state or as a slave state. The South wanted Missouri to enter as a slave state. This meant that the South would have more votes in Congress and slavery could continue to grow. The North wanted Missouri to enter the Union as a free state so that the spread of slavery could be stopped. Each side was anxious to claim Missouri. The problem was solved when Maine applied for admission to the Union as a free state. Congress then gave Maine the right to enter the Union as a free state and Missouri could enter as a slave state. However, Congress stated that other new states to be formed out of new areas north of a specific line would not be permitted to enter as slave states. They would enter as free states. This agreement satisfied both the North and South. It was called the Missouri Compromise.

The Compromise of 1850

In 1849 gold was discovered in California. Many people rushed to California to find their fortune in gold. Soon the California area had enough people to become a state. The people in California wanted to become a free state. The southern states became angry. They did not want California to enter the Union as a free state. To do so would upset the balance of twelve free states and twelve slave states.

Southerners felt that the northern states would gain more voting power to further block slavery in other new territories. If the South could claim California as a slave state, they would have more voting power in the Congress and slavery would continue to spread. Bitter debates arose in the Congress. South Carolina and other southern states threatened to leave the Union if California joined as a free state. Several other problems arose. One was the underground railroad. Southerners felt that the North was stealing their property when runaway slaves using secret hiding places were permitted to remain in the North. Southerners demanded a stricter fugitive slave law. Another issue was slavery in Washington, D.C., the nation's capital. These problems were threatening to split the nation.

In 1850 Henry Clay, a lawmaker in Congress, proposed a solution to the problem. He suggested a set of laws that were known as the Compromise of 1850. One of the laws stated that California could enter as a free state. Fugitive slave laws provided for the return of runaway slaves who escaped from one state to another. One law stated that slaves who ran away to the North or other free states could be captured and returned to their masters. The slaves would be arrested by government officials. Anyone who helped slaves escape would have to pay a fine of $1000. Rewards were offered for run-away slaves. This made northerners and abolitionists (those who opposed slavery) very angry. Many northern states passed personal liberty laws that prohibited state and local officers from obeying the national fugitive slave law.

The conflict of slavery caused a major conflict between the northern and southern states. What started out as a compromise or an agreement had become a major disagreement. The nation was headed for a civil war.

What's Happening?

Listed below are events described in the Missouri Compromise and the Compromise of 1850 on the preceding pages. Place these events in sequential order by writing the event in its correct place.

Example:

1. <u>Missouri applied for admission to the Union.</u>

2. _____

3. _____

4. _____

5. _____

6. _____

7. _____

8. _____

9. _____

10. _____

Events: The nation was headed for a civil war.

Henry Clay proposed a solution to the problem between the northern and southern states.

The Missouri Compromise

Maine applied for admission to the Union.

Northerners became angry.

The Compromise of 1850

Bitter debate arose in Congress.

Personal liberty laws were passed.

Gold was discovered in California.

The Kansas-Nebraska Act

In 1854 something happened that really pleased the South. Senator Stephen A. Douglas of Illinois introduced to Congress a bill called the Kansas-Nebraska Act. The bill was designed to win the support of the southern congressmen. This act said that settlers in the new Louisiana Territory would have the right to decide by vote as to whether or not they wanted slavery.

The Kansas-Nebraska Act replaced the Missouri Compromise in which the Congress decided whether to admit states carved out of new territory. It gave states popular sovereignty. This meant the people of Nebraska and Kansas could decide for themselves whether or not they wanted slavery.

Most northerners thought that slavery was evil. They did not want to add more slave states to the Union. There was a bitter fight in Congress, but the bill was passed. President Franklin Pierce supported the bill and it became law. Many southerners moved quickly to Kansas and so did many antislavery northerners.

If enough northerners settled in the Kansas-Nebraska area, they could vote slavery out. On the other hand if more southerners settled in the area, they could vote to have slavery. Tension began to rise between the two groups. Finally it reached its peak in Kansas. The two sides clashed in a bloody fight. Over two hundred people were killed. After this the Kansas territory became known as "Bleeding Kansas."

There was no such fighting in the Nebraska area. It was widely accepted that it would enter the Union as a free state. The Kansas-Nebraska Act caused more bitter quarrels between the northern and southern states. This moved the states closer than ever to the brink of war.

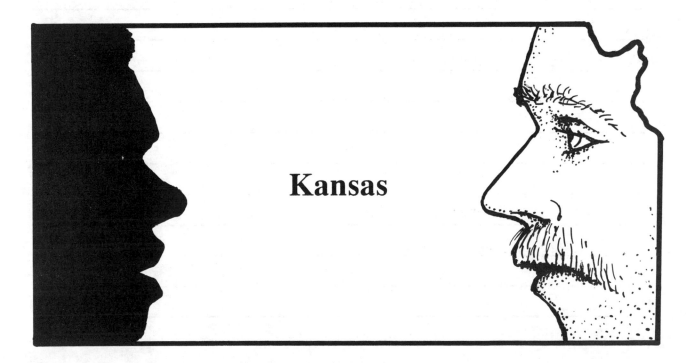

Kansas

Tell It!

Explain the Kansas-Nebraska Act to a friend. Write your explanation in the space below.

_____

_____

_____

_____

_____

_____

_____

_____

_____

_____

_____

How was the Kansas-Nebraska Act different from the Missouri Compromise? Write your answer in the space below.

_____

_____

_____

_____

_____

_____

_____

_____

_____

GA1345

The Civil War Era

The firing of the first shots that crashed into Fort Sumter at 4:30 a.m. on April 12, 1861, started the bloodiest war in American history. It was called the Civil War or the War Between the States. Of all the wars that Americans have fought, the Civil War is the war that most people have read about. Even today the Civil War lives on in the hearts and minds of American people. Each year hundreds of people put on uniforms and reenact the Civil War for audiences in many places throughout the United States.

In 1990 a new Civil War movie was released. It was called *Glory*. Black actors Morgan Freeman and Denzel Washington starred in the movie. It was a film about the all black 54th Regiment of Massachusetts. Americans were fascinated by the movie. They flocked to the movie theaters in large numbers. Perhaps you have read about the Civil War or have studied it at school. But you probably have not studied the role that black Americans played in the war.

For a while it seemed that they would not be allowed to fight for their country. The Civil War began in 1861, but it was late in 1862 before Blacks were allowed to fight. African Americans did not cause the Civil War, but the war was fought because of them.

In 1860 Abraham Lincoln became the sixteenth president of the United States. He was a Republican. The Republican party promised that slavery would not be permitted in the northern territories. They also promised that escaped slaves would not be sent back South without jury trials. This made the people in the South angry. They feared that the Republicans were forcing them to change their way of life that depended on slave labor in the cotton and tobacco fields.

Eleven southern states withdrew from the Union. South Carolina was the first to withdraw. It was followed by Virginia, North Carolina, Georgia, Florida, Mississippi, Alabama, Tennessee, Arkansas, Louisiana and Texas.

In February of 1861, delegates from these states met in Montgomery, Alabama, and formed the Confederate States of America. They elected Jefferson Davis as their president. Their capital was located first at Montgomery; later it was moved to Richmond, Virginia.

President Lincoln felt that a war was about to begin. In April 1861 he sent supplies to Fort Sumter at Charleston, South Carolina. Confederate soldiers began firing on the fort at 4:30 in the morning. The Civil War had begun!

Many Blacks in the free states went to enlist in the Union Army, but they were turned away. President Lincoln feared that if Blacks were allowed to join the Union Army, the border slave states of Delaware, Maryland, Kentucky and Missouri would join the Confederacy. Frederick Douglass and other abolitionists pleaded with President Lincoln to free the slaves in the Confederate states and enlist black troops in the Union Army.

At first Lincoln would not listen; the war raged on. The Union soldiers were growing tired of the war. Few were volunteering to fight. Many had been killed or injured in the war. The Union Army was losing more battles than it was winning.

In July of 1862, Congress passed two laws. One was the Confiscation Act. It declared that if a slave owner helped the Confederacy, his slaves would go free. The other law was called the Militia Act. It gave the president the power to use Blacks as soldiers. As Northern armies drove into Confederate territories, slaves in the Confederate states fled and joined the Union Army. They were called contraband and considered to be tools just as guns and ammunition seized from the enemy. They were not to be returned.

On New Year's Day in 1863, President Lincoln issued the Emancipation Proclamation. The Emancipation Proclamation stated that slaves in states or districts in rebellion against the United States on January 1, 1863, would be "thenceforth and forever free." Five days after the Proclamation was issued, the first regiment of black soldiers entered the Union Army. Thousands of free Blacks rushed to join the Union Army. These fresh new troops gave the Union Army new strength and victories.

The war dragged on for another two years, but Abraham Lincoln's Emancipation Proclamation was the first major step in bringing an end to slavery and the Civil War.

Words, Words, Words

Use the letters in the words *Emancipation Proclamation* to make as many words as you can. Write your words in the correct spaces on the chart below.

2-letter words	3-letter words	4-letter words	5-letter words	6-letter words

Use your chart to answer these questions.

1. For which group did you have the largest number of words? _____

2. For which group did you have the smallest number of words? _____

3. How many five-letter words did you make? _____

4. How many four-letter words did you make? _____

5. How many six-letter words did you make? _____

GA1345

The Lineup

The eighteen states of the Union are listed on the left of the trench. List the eleven Confederate states on the right side of the trench. List the border states in the trench.

1. Maine
2. New Hampshire
3. Vermont
4. Massachusetts
5. Rhode Island
6. Connecticut
7. New York
8. New Jersey
9. Pennsylvania
10. Ohio
11. Michigan
12. Indiana
13. Illinois
14. Wisconsin
15. Minnesota
16. Iowa
17. Oregon
18. California

1. _____
2. _____
3. _____
4. _____
5. _____
6. _____
7. _____
8. _____
9. _____
10. _____
11. _____

Map Activity

Use the key below to color regions of the map.

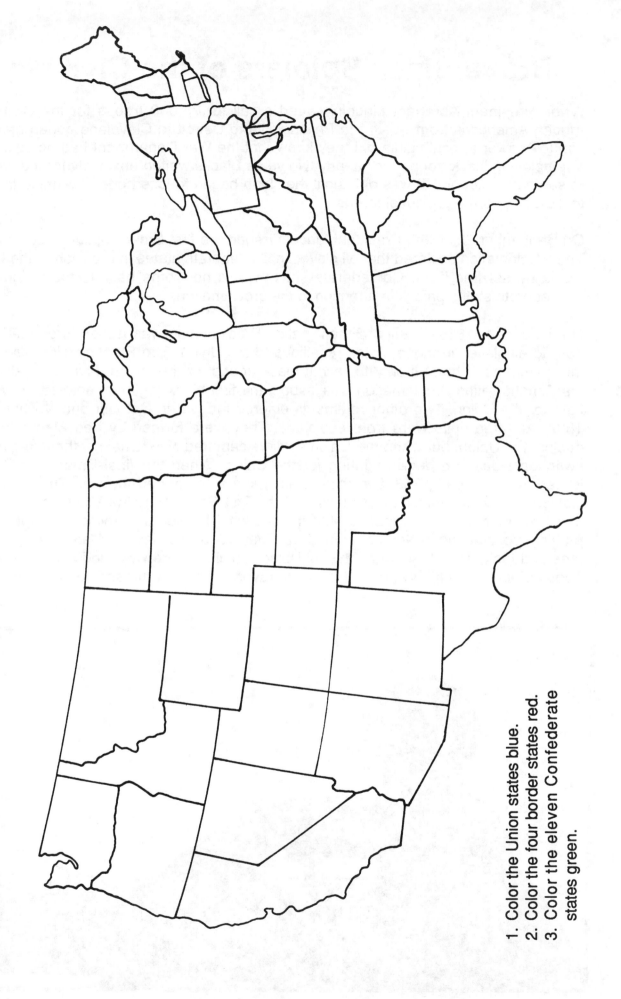

1. Color the Union states blue.
2. Color the four border states red.
3. Color the eleven Confederate states green.

GA1345

Brave Black Soldiers of the Civil War

When President Abraham Lincoln issued a call for 75,000 troops for the Civil War, African Americans from Boston to Philadelphia to Detroit to Cleveland began preparation to answer the call. Little did they know that the War Department had no intentions of employing black troops. For nearly two years Blacks waited anxiously for the chance to serve their country. It was only until the North began to lose hope of winning the war that black troops were considered.

On September 22, 1862, President Lincoln issued the first Emancipation Proclamation. The proclamation declared that all slaves in Confederate states in rebellion to the Union would be set free if the Confederate states would not come back to the Union. The Confederate states paid little attention to the proclamation.

On January 1, 1863, the final Emancipation Proclamation was issued. It granted freedom to all slaves in those states rebellious to the Union. The Emancipation also gave the government the authority to recruit black troops for the Union. Five days after the first Emancipation Proclamation was issued, the first black regiment entered the war to fight for the Union. Two other regiments entered the war in October and November of 1862. All three units were from Louisiana. They were formed by free Blacks to fight against the Union; but when the Union soldiers captured New Orleans, these regiments switched sides and began fighting for the Union. When the final Emancipation was issued in January of 1863, two more black regiments entered the war. They were the first colored volunteers from Kansas and the first South Carolina Volunteers. Both of these regiments were composed of former slaves. The South Carolina Volunteers took part in a coastal raid in November of 1862. They freed 155 slaves, killed nine Confederates and took three prisoners. Only four black soldiers were wounded and none killed. These Blacks were highly praised for their bravery by their commanding officers.

Over one million Blacks fled the Confederacy and joined the Union Army, when the Union came near enough for them to escape. They served the Union army as laborers and spies.

More than 200,000 Blacks from the North and the South enrolled in the Union Army and Navy. Of the 186,000 black soldiers in the Union Army, 133,000 had been slaves in the southern states. Fifty-three thousand were free Northern Blacks. The first regiments of free Blacks in the North were the 54th and 55th Massachusetts.

Thirty thousand Blacks served in the Union Navy. Black sailors served along with white sailors on an equal basis. This was not the case in the Union Army. Black soldiers in the Union Army were not treated fairly by the government. White soldiers were paid $10.00 a month and $3.50 for food and clothing. Blacks received only $7.00 a month. Three dollars were taken out of their checks for food and clothing. Black soldiers received less training than white soldiers. Black troops had to serve longer terms than white troops. They had no chance of advancement. Black troops worked with poor equipment and had low-quality food.

Despite all of the problems that black soldiers faced during the war, they proved themselves to be highly capable and courageous in battle. On five hundred battlefields from Mississippi to Virginia they fought.

When Secretary of War Edwin Stanton made a report to President Lincoln about the war, he stated that the black soldiers "have proved themselves among the bravest of the brave, performing daring deeds and shedding their blood with a heroism unsurpassed by soldiers of any race." The Union had finally realized that black soldiers could fight and that many were willing to give their lives to defend their country.

Throughout the war Blacks distinguished themselves as brave and courageous soldiers.

GA1345

Black Medal of Honor Winners

One of the first ideas for giving a medal to brave soldiers came from George Washington. In 1782 he issued an order that any soldier who showed outstanding bravery should be permitted to wear on his left breast the figure of a heart made of purple cloth. This was the beginning of the Purple Heart medal. Only three Purple Hearts were awarded; then the idea was dropped. Then Napoleon Bonaparte, the French ruler, wanted something that would give soldiers the urge to fight bravely until death. He was the ruler who wanted to conquer all Europe. He knew that he needed soldiers who were as brave as could be. So he came up with the idea of an award for soldiers that would face the most disastrous situations and not give up. He would give them an award called the Legion of Honor.

Soon other countries wanted to give awards to their brave soldiers, too. In England soldiers were given the Victoria Cross. Brave German soldiers were awarded the Iron Cross. Russians awarded the Cross of St. George to its brave soldiers. The United States had no symbol or award to give brave men who gave their lives to defend their country. Three Purple Hearts and six special medals were awarded during the Revolutionary War. Besides these medals, no others were given in any other early wars. Many brave soldiers who had fought in these wars were not recognized. Most people felt that since Europe was giving medals, Americans should not give medals because it would seem that the United States would be copying their idea.

In 1862, one year after the Civil War began, Congress felt that America's soldiers should have something to show for their brave actions. So Congress passed two bills creating Medals of Honor, one for the Army and one for the Navy. The U.S. Medal of Honor is not given for ordinary bravery. All soldiers are ordinarily brave. It is given to the bravest of the brave soldiers, one who goes over and beyond the call of duty. Other medals for bravery include the Distinguished Service Cross, the Distinguished Service Medal and the Purple Heart.

The Medal of Honor is the highest award given to members of the armed forces. It is not pinned to the chest as other medals are. It is worn around the neck on a blue ribbon with stars. Few medal winners ever wear the medal. They usually wear little cloth bars or cloth rosettes to show that they are medal winners.

During the Civil War twenty-three black soldiers were awarded the Medal of Honor for bravery. Sergeant William Carney was the first black man to win the Medal of Honor. Other black army soldiers who won Medals of Honor were Private William Barnes, First Sergeant James Bronson, First Sergeant Powhatan Beaty, Sergeant Decatur Dorsey, Sergeant Major Christian A. Fleetwood, Private James Gardiner, Sergeant James Harris, Sergeant Major Thomas Hawkins, Sergeant Alfred Hilton, Sergeant Major Milton Holland, Corporal Miles James, First Sergeant Alexander Kelly, First Sergeant Robert Pinn, First Sergeant Edward Ratcliff and Private Charles Veal. Navy Medal of Honor winners were Aaron Anderson, Robert Blake, William Brown, Wilson Brown, James Mifflin, Joachin Pease and John Lawson.

Find the Winners

During the Civil War twenty-three black soldiers won the nation's highest military award—the Medal of Honor. Find twenty-two of the last names of the soldiers in the puzzle below. Write the missing soldier's first name in the blank space below.

```
N K Y D X S Z S M O V L S C E X G Y F O X
B Q V W E P Q H K Q L Z R P D P Q I S L M
E L E M B L I X L U Z N Z E F Y M S L U Q
S T A W F L B N S P S I Y F C M Z G W W V
Z J L K S Z I R N B V Q I O I I T H L U L
X H L P E A S E I E B L X F A N I T R P I
U P H I L T O N K A C J F Y X A X D K O X
D L F O H S W I W T H L B H I U V D F Z R
Z U T I C Y V D A Y I G Q H H T N E B X Y
L X F D Z S C R H N H M H N D Q N E J V N
D Q L N O S W A L F D O H W Y D I K A M P
Q T J F Y G R G U F L E E T W O O D D M T
D E B H E R K E L L Y D R M Y N U Z J Y M
N M S K I C P F A H Y O B S W Q B O L D G
B H M S D W R N S E N R A B O Y U R C X H
E A S A N Z D V N K O S V Z X N H Q O H I
I K D H Z G Q R H W T E T T D Z Z X C W V
H A J U J H A H N G T Y E T Q S P Y J E N
E Z X L V C A G E L M A S E M N Y V Z O E
```

1. _____ Fleetwood
2. _____ Gardiner
3. _____ Brown
4. _____ Lawson
5. _____ Dorsey
6. _____ Pease
7. _____ James
8. _____ Pinn

9. _____ Anderson
10. _____ Mifflin
11. _____ Holland
12. _____ Hilton
13. _____ Barnes
14. _____ Blake
15. _____ Beaty
16. _____ Ratcliff

17. _____ Brown
18. _____ Hawkins
19. _____ Harris
20. _____ Carney
21. _____ Kelly
22. _____ Veal

Facts and Figures of the Civil War

Write the numerical equivalents next to the underlined number words in each of the statements below. Use the scale at the right. The first statement is done for you.

1. When the Civil War began, the total population of the United States was about <u>thirty-one million, four hundred forty-three thousand</u> (31,443,000).

Millions	Hundred Thousands	Ten Thousands	Thousands	Hundreds	Tens	Ones
31	4	4	3	0	0	0

2. When the Civil War began, there were more than <u>four million, four hundred forty-one thousand</u> (   ) African Americans in the United States.

3. The Confederates used <u>three million, five hundred thousand</u> (   ) slaves to work in factories and fields to produce goods for the Confederate Army.

4. At the beginning of the war, the Union had <u>twenty-two million</u> (   )people.

5. The South had only <u>nine million</u>(   ) people.

6. More than <u>two hundred thousand</u> (   ) Blacks from the North and South enrolled in the Union Army and Navy.

7. Of the Union's <u>one hundred eighty-six thousand</u> (   ) black soldiers, <u>one hundred thirty-three thousand</u> (   ) were former southern slaves.

8. <u>Thirty thousand</u> (   ) Blacks served in the Union Navy.

9. When the Emancipation Proclamation freed slaves in states in rebellion to the Union, some <u>eight hundred thousand</u> (   ) slaves remained in bondage.

10. Five slave states on the Union side had <u>four hundred fifty thousand</u> (   ) slaves.

Civil War Task Cards

Christian A. Fleetwood

Christian Fleetwood was a black man of superior intelligence. He was born in Baltimore, Maryland, and grew up in the household of John Brune, a wealthy sugar merchant. At the age of sixteen, he was sent on a business trip to Africa for the Brune Sugar Company. He later attended Ashmun Institute, now Lincoln University in Pennsylvania. When Christian grew up he joined the Union Army with the 4th Regiment of Baltimore. In September of 1864, the 4th Regiment fought at Fort Gilmer, Richmond, Virginia. It is here that Christian A. Fleetwood and Alfred Hinton, another brave black soldier, were awarded Congressional Medals of Honor for bravely rescuing the American flag.

Christian A. Fleetwood was a black man of superior intelligence.

A. Tell what you think this means.

B. List ten other African Americans (past or present) who showed superior intelligence.

Dr. Alexander T. Augusta

Dr. Alexander T. Augusta was a medical doctor and surgeon for the 7th Colored Regiment of Maryland. He was born in Norfolk, Virginia, and received his medical degree from Trinity College in Toronto, Canada. He was in charge of examining black recruits. In later years he operated an Army hospital in Savannah, Georgia. After the Civil War, he was promoted to lieutenant colonel, the highest rank achieved by any black soldier in the Union Army.

Once when Dr. Augusta was promoted to a position over two white assistants, they became angry. They did not want to work under a black man. To solve the problem, Dr. Augusta was transferred to another job. Do you think that this was fair? List other ways that this problem might have been solved.

GA1345

James Lewis

The Civil War battle at Port Hudson, Louisiana, was one of the major battles in which black troops fought. During this battle, James Lewis became a hero. At the outbreak of the Civil War, James Lewis served as an officer for the Confederacy. When the Union took New Orleans, Lewis switched sides and began fighting for the Union Army. He was one of the first persons to raise up two companies of black troops. He later became captain of the 1st Regiment of Louisiana. When the war ended he worked for the federal government to help set up schools for former slaves. Afterwards, he held other government positions.

In 1867 he was appointed U.S. Custom Inspector.

In 1869 he was a member of the New Orleans police department.

In 1870 he was Administrator of Police and Colonel in the 2nd Regiment of the State Militia.

In 1872 he was Administrator of Public Improvements for the City of New Orleans. It is said that he saved the city a half million dollars during his first year in office. He later became involved in politics and represented Louisiana at a Republican Convention.

In 1884 he was appointed surveyor general of the state of Louisiana.

A. Make a time line to show events and dates in the life of James Lewis.

William Harvey Carney

In early 1863 William Carney was twenty-three years old. He enlisted in the Morgan Guards which later became part of the 54th Regiment of Massachusetts. In July of 1863, the 54th was involved in a battle where Carney performed a daring and brave deed. When a color guard (a color guard bears the flag in battle) fell in the battle, Carney rushed through a volley of enemy bullets to rescue the American flag. When the act was completed, Carney yelled, "The old flag never touched the ground." As he handed it to a standing soldier, he sank to the ground, weak from the wounds that he had received while trying to rescue the flag. The flag that Carney rescued is displayed in Memorial Hall in Boston, Massachusetts.

William Carney believed that the United States flag was very important. He was willing to give his life for it. List ten things that are very important to you.

GA1345

The Robert Smalls Story

Have you ever been made to do something that you did not want to do but found out later that you were glad that you had done it? Such was the case with Robert Smalls. He was born a slave in Beaufort, South Carolina, in 1839. He became an expert pilot on boats in and around the Charleston, North Carolina, harbor. During the Civil War he was forced to pilot a warship for the Confederacy called the *Planter*. Robert Smalls was a twenty-three-year-old slave. He could not read or write. But he became an expert in piloting the *Planter*. To those around him, Smalls appeared to be just another hard-working slave. No one had any idea of his planned escape using the *Planter*. One morning in May of 1862, Robert Smalls used his knowledge to pilot himself and several other black Americans to freedom. That morning Smalls had dressed himself as the captain of the ship. He steered it out of the Confederate territory to the Union. No one became suspicious at first because the *Planter* had been scheduled to leave early that morning. The twenty-men team of guards saw the ship pull out at 3:00 a.m. with what looked like Confederate Commander General Roswell Ripley.

Later it was found that the Commander had not been with the *Planter*. No one had any idea of what had happened. The *Planter* was a very valuable ship to the Confederacy. It had a cannon gun that could pivot and fire from any direction, other guns and a large supply of ammunition. When the Commander realized that no one knew why the ship was missing, he became furious and ordered a search for it.

In the meantime the *Planter* was reaching the Union. When Union forces recognized a Confederacy ship drifting into their territory, they made preparations to fire on the ship. But through the fog a sailor spotted a white sheet waving in the wind. Fire was withheld. As the *Planter* guided closer, they spotted a black man wearing the hat and jacket of a Confederate ship captain. "Good morning, Sir," Robert Smalls said. "I have brought you some of the old United States guns." On the *Planter's* deck was Robert Smalls and seven other black men. From down below inside the ship came eight more slaves, five women, two children and a baby.

In addition to gaining freedom for himself, his family and friends, Smalls had delivered a valuable ship to the Union. He also brought valuable information. He knew where torpedoes and traps had been placed in the rivers and creeks. In the ship's cabin was a book containing the secret meanings of the Confederate flags and signals.

When the *New York Times* got the news, they called it "one of the most heroic acts of the Civil War." After this daring act, Smalls piloted the *Planter* for the Union during the Civil War.

When the Civil War was over, Smalls settled in Beaufort where he grew up. In fact, Smalls purchased his former master's house and the slave living quarters where Smalls was born. In later years Smalls learned to read and write. He became a political leader in South Carolina. From 1868 to 1875 he served in the South Carolina legislature and in the U.S. House of Representatives from 1875 to 1879. In 1879 a special statute (law) provided Smalls with a pension.

In 1900 the United States Congress recorded a statute providing a reward for Robert Smalls, the hero. The statute read, "Robert Smalls, on the thirteenth day of May eighteen hundred and sixty-two, did capture the steamer *Planter* with all the armament and ammunition for Fort Ripley at the city of Charleston taking her out and turning her over to the federal Blockading Squadron off Charleston."

In 1890, Republican President Benjamin Harrison appointed Smalls Collector of the Port of Beaufort. Smalls held that post until 1913. Robert Smalls died in 1915.

In recent years the state government placed a marker, relating the act, at a churchyard in Beaufort where Smalls was buried.

GA1345

No Small Matter

The Confederacy forced a slave named Robert Smalls to learn to pilot a large warship called the *Planter*. When he had learned enough, he guided the ship away from the Confederacy and turned it over to the Union. By doing this he became a hero and won freedom for himself and others.

Listed below are ten chores/tasks that your parents say you must do. Opposite of each task, write something that you could learn from doing the task.

Task

What I Could Learn from It

Example:

1. Wash dishes ———— I could learn to be clean. ————

2. Make your bed ——————————————————

3. Do homework ——————————————————

4. Play the piano ——————————————————

5. Get to school on time ——————————————————

6. Hang up your clothes ——————————————————

7. Feed the dog ——————————————————

8. Go to bed on time ——————————————————

9. Water the houseplants ——————————————————

10. Take a shower/bath ——————————————————

GA1345

Small Spots

Use crayons to color the information spots about Robert Smalls. Cut the spots out and glue them in the correct order on the following page.

Birth date of Robert Smalls

Date that Robert Smalls died

Robert Smalls piloted himself and others to freedom.

Robert Smalls served in the South Carolina Legislature.

Robert Smalls represented South Carolina in the U.S. House of Representatives.

Robert Smalls was appointed Collector of the Port of Beaufort.

Robert Smalls' junior high school in Beaufort, South Carolina, stands as a memorial.

A special statute (law) provided Smalls with a pension.

The U.S. Congress recorded a statute providing a reward for Mr. Smalls.

Robert Smalls post as Collector of the Port of Beaufort ended.

Small Spots

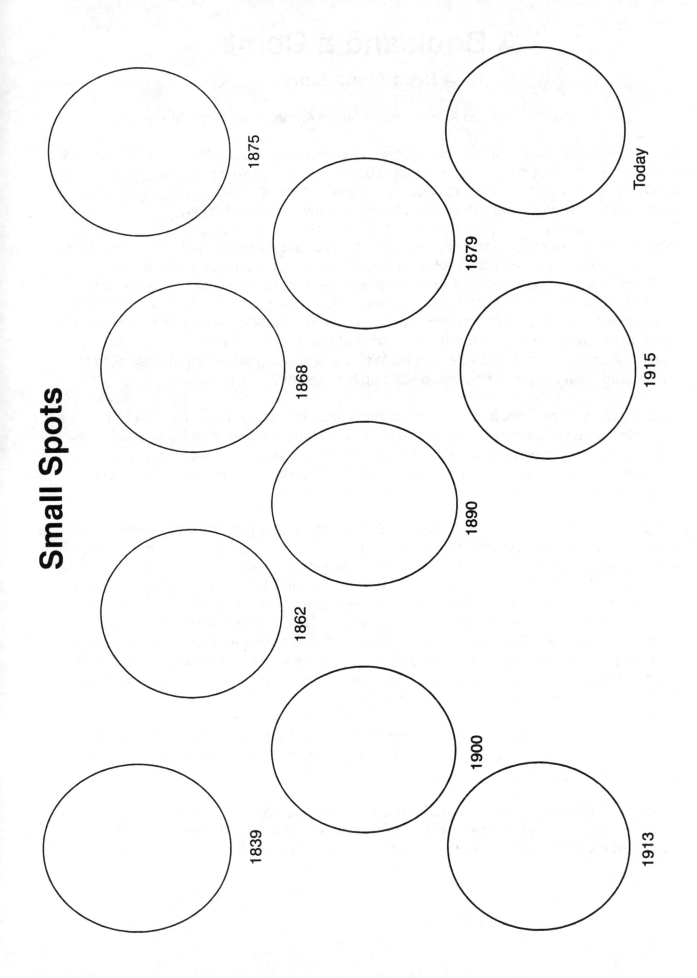

1875

Today

1879

1868

1915

1890

1862

1839

1900

1913

A Book and a Comb

A Read-Aloud Story

Adapted from Allen Allensworth: Man of Ambition *by Ruth Pitman*

Allen Allensworth was a small boy living with his mother in Louisville, Kentucky, when it was discovered that his master's young son was teaching Allen to read. Rules were harsh for slaves who learned to read. Any slave who was caught learning to read or write was punished. Usually this meant being sold away from his family.

When Allen was eleven years old, it was discovered that he could read. Allen was taken from his mother and sold to a tobacco plantation owner far away from his mother in Louisville. As he said good-bye to his mother, she pressed a silver half dollar into his hand. With tears in her eyes she whispered, "Allen, buy yourself a book and a comb." She told him to buy a comb to keep his hair neat and a book to continue his reading. As soon as he arrived at his new mistress' home she took away his comb. She said that it was too nice for a slave, but Allen hid his Webster's spelling book before she could take it and used it every spare moment to keep up his reading.

After a year of hard work and harsh treatment, Allen ran away. Twice he tried to escape and twice he was returned to his mistress. A slave who continued to try to escape was often considered a troublemaker and was often sold away. This was the fate of Allen Allensworth. This time he was sold to a racehorse owner in New Orleans, Louisiana, where he was trained to be a jockey to ride racehorses.

In 1861 when Allen was nineteen years old, his master sent him back to Louisville, Kentucky, at the Oakland Race Course. Because of the upcoming Civil War, the race was not held as planned; instead Allen and other black jockeys were sent to a farm to work. The overseer of the farm was cruel and the work was hard, but Allen was a good worker. He was soon sent to an estate near Louisville to work as a house servant. Soon after his arrival at the estate, the Civil War began. Union troops surrounded the estate where Allen worked. One day one of the Union officers asked Allen to come with him to be a nurse helper for the hospital corp of the Union Army. He would serve with the 44th Infantry Volunteer Division from Illinois. At last Allen was free. Slaves who signed up to serve in the Union Army were granted their freedom.

When Allen returned to Ohio with the Infantry, he decided to join the Navy. It was the only service that admitted Blacks. During his stay in the Navy, he earned the rank of first-class petty officer.

When the war ended, Allen got a job in a naval supply yard in St. Louis, Missouri. He saved his money and opened up two restaurants in partnership with his brother. He soon sold his interest in the restaurant and returned to Louisville.

GA1345

At the age of twenty-five Allen attended school and worked as a janitor. He did so well in his studies that the Freedmen's Bureau hired him to teach in a small school. The Freedmen's Bureau was established by Congress to help restore the South after the Civil War. In 1871 Allen was ordained a minister to preach the Gospel. To prepare himself as a minister, Allen attended the Baptist Theological Institute, now the Roger Williams University. Years later he was awarded the honorary master of arts degree from this institution.

In 1880 and 1884 Allen became the only black delegate to the Republican National Convention. In 1882 white chaplains (ministers) served all of the black army units. Allen thought that black soldiers should be served by a black chaplain. He knew that his religious training qualified him for the job. In 1886 when a vacancy occurred, Allen wrote a letter to President Grover Cleveland asking that he be considered for the job. In April of that year the president assigned Allen as Chaplain of the 24th Infantry.

His twenty-year job as chaplain took him to New Mexico, Utah, Montana and California. During these twenty years he taught his troops vocational skills such as printing, baking and telegraphy. He also taught classes in grammar and history.

When his Infantry fought in the Philippines, Allen started a school there teaching skills that black soldiers needed to make them better soldiers. When he retired in 1906, Allen had advanced to the rank of lieutenant colonel. He then returned his attention to fulfill a dream that he had always had. He wanted to build a community of black citizens where he and other Blacks could live and work without racial prejudice. Together with four other friends, Allen formed the California Colony and Home Promotion Association. They bought twenty acres in the fertile San Joaquin Valley. There he founded the small town and community of Allensworth, California. Then problems arose. The water company refused to supply ample water for the town which had now expanded to eighty acres. The water company had gone back on its promise to supply the growing town with water.

Before the problem was solved, Allen was killed in a motorcycle accident in 1914. He didn't live to see his dream come true, but today he has not been forgotten, for his town is being reconstructed. The town of Allensworth, California, now stands as a tribute to a man who believed in God, one who believed in others and one who believed in himself. He had the courage and determination to use a book and a comb to propel himself to freedom, education and dignity.

GA1345

Battle Hymns and Camp Songs

For the black soldier, fighting in the Civil War brought much pain, suffering and sorrow; but many found some consolation and comfort in battle hymns and camp songs that they sang.

One of the favorite camp songs was "Rally, Boys, Rally."

Rally, Boys, Rally

So rally, boys, rally, let us never mind the past.
We had a hard road to travel, but our day is coming fast.

For God is for the right, and we have no need to fear,–

The Union must be saved by the Colored Volunteer.

One of the favorite marching songs for the 1st Arkansas unit was "Many Thousand Gone."

Many Thousand Gone

No more auction block for me,
No more, no more,
No more auction block for me,
Many thousand gone.

No more drivers' lash for me,
No more, no more,
No more drivers' lash for me,
Many thousand gone.

No more peck of salt for me,
No more, no more,
No more peck of salt for me,
Many thousand gone.

No more iron chain for me,
No more, no more,
No more iron chain for me,
Many thousand gone.

This marching song of the 1st Arkansas was sung to the tune of "John Brown's Body." It was the fighting song of the 1st Arkansas Colored Regiment of the Union Army.

Oh, we're bully soldiers of the "First Arkansas."
We are fighting for the Union; we are fighting for the law,
We can hit a rebel further than a white man ever saw,
As we go marching on.

CHORUS:
    Glory, glory, hallelujah,
    Glory, glory, hallelujah,
    Glory, glory, hallelujah,
    As we go marching on.

See, there above the center, where the flag is waving bright.
We are going out of slavery; we're bound for freedom's light;
We mean to show Jeff Davis how the African can fight,
As we go marching on.

We have done with hoeing cotton; we have done with hoeing corn.
We are colored Yankee soldiers, now, as sure as you are born;
When the Master hears us yelling, they'll think it's Gabriel's horn,
As we go marching on.

They will have to pay us wages, the wages of their sin,
They will have to bow their foreheads to their colored kith and kin,
They will have to give us house room, or the roof shall tumble in!
As we go marching on.

They say, "Now colored brethren, you shall be forever free
From the first of January, eighteen hundred sixty-three."
We have heard it in the river going rushing to the sea,
As it went sounding on.

Father Abraham has spoken and the message has been sent;
The prison doors he opened and out the prisons went,
To join the sable army of African descent,
As we go marching on.

GA1345

Battle Hymn of the Republic

Mine eyes have seen the glory of the coming of the Lord;
He is trampling out the vintage where the grapes of wrath are stored;
He hath loosed the fateful lightning of his terrible swift sword:
His truth is marching on.

CHORUS:
    Glory, glory, hallelujah!
    Glory, glory, hallelujah!
    Glory, glory, hallelujah!
    His truth is marching on!

"Battle Hymn of the Republic" is one of the most widely sung American patriotic songs. It was written by Julia Ward Howe. Julia Howe and her husband were active in the abolition and women's rights movements. She wrote the "Battle Hymn of the Republic" shortly after she visited a Union Army camp near Washington, D.C. This stirring battle hymn was written to the tune of an old Sunday school song. It was a popular battle hymn among the Civil War soldiers of the Union.

"John Brown's Body" was another popular song sung by soldiers as they marched into battle during the Civil War. It has the same tune as the "Battle Hymn of the Republic." It was written to sing the praises of John Brown, a white abolitionist who gave his life in an effort to use guerrilla warfare to free slaves and advance the abolition movement.

These are the words of the first two verses and chorus of the John Brown song.

John Brown's body lies amouldering in the grave,
John Brown's body lies amouldering in the grave,
John Brown's body lies amouldering in the grave,
His soul goes marching on!

He's gone to be a soldier in the Army of the Lord,
He's gone to be a soldier in the Army of the Lord,
He's gone to be a soldier in the Army of the Lord,
His soul goes marching on!

    Glory, glory, hallelujah!
    Glory, glory, hallelujah!
    Glory, glory, hallelujah!
    His soul is marching on!

Let's Sing

Copy the first verse and chorus of the "Battle Hymn of the Republic." Then research one or two more verses and write them. Now copy John Brown's song. Organize your class and sing both songs.

The Battle of the Crater

In June 1864, Ulysses S. Grant, a Union general, began a ten-month siege of the city of Petersburg, Virginia. The Confederate General Robert E. Lee was defending the city. A group of miners suggested a plan of attack to take the city. They suggested that a tunnel could be dug under the Confederate battle line. Gunpowder would be placed in the tunnel and lit with a long fuse. The explosion would blow a large hole in the Confederate defenses and surprise them. Then Union soldiers could attack. The suggestion was taken and plans began immediately for digging the tunnel.

One of the two African American divisions serving with General Grant was to lead the attack. The 4th Division led by white officer Brigadier General Edward Ferrero was selected to lead the attack. The 4th Division was selected because those soldiers were rested. While the tunnel was being dug, the black soldiers practiced and prepared for the attack. After three weeks the tunnel was finished. It stretched 511 feet from the Union lines to the Confederate line. Two additional tunnels 38 feet each were dug on each side of the main tunnel. Eight small tunnels extended from the side tunnels. They were filled with four tons of gunpowder.

July 30, 1864, had been set as the date to set off the explosion, but at the last minute a big change was made. Instead of using the already trained black troops, plans were made to use white troops instead. When the fuse was ignited, the gunpowder-filled tunnels exploded leaving a great crater (hole) in the earth. It measured 30 feet deep and 60 feet wide. The white troops moved in but because they were not trained, they were unable to break through the Confederate line. Finally black troops were sent in, but it was too late. The Confederate troops drove the black troops back. The 43rd United States Colored Troops captured the Confederate flags. It was all in vain because at 10:00 a.m. General Grant ordered a retreat of all Union soldiers. The Battle of the Crater had failed. General Grant explained why the black troops were not put up front. "It would have been said that they were shoving black troops to be killed because no one cared about their lives." General Grant admitted that it was a mistake not to use the already trained black troops. He stated that if he had used the original plan to have the black troops move in first that the Battle of the Crater would have been a success.

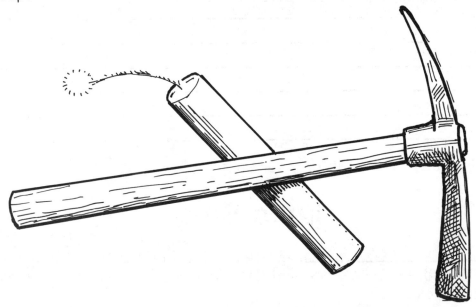

Apologize

You are Union General Ulysses S. Grant. Write a letter of apology to the black troops for not being used as planned in the Battle of the Crater.

_____

_____

_____

_____

_____

_____

_____

_____

_____

_____

_____

_____

_____

_____

_____

_____

_____

_____

_____

_____

_____

_____

Sincerely,

_____
  (your name)

GA1345

Constitutional Amendments

When the Civil War had ended, there were many problems to be solved. One of the problems was that of ex-slaves. Should they be granted the rights that other United States citizens had? This problem was solved when Congress passed three amendments to the Constitution.

The first of these was the 13th Amendment. It was passed in 1865. The 13th Amendment freed all slaves. It said that slavery shall not exist within the United States of America. Three years later, Congress passed the 14th Amendment. It made Blacks United States citizens. It gave all persons equal protection under the law. It said that the states could not take away a citizen's right to life, liberty or property without due process.

In 1870 Congress passed another amendment. The 15th Amendment gave Blacks the right to vote. It said a citizen's right to vote shall not be denied due to race, color or previous servitude.

Imaginary Amendment

Write an amendment to one of your classroom rules. Write the rule on the first line. Write an amendment for the rule on the second line.

Example:

Rule: No student shall chew gum in class.

Amendment: A student shall be permitted to chew gum in class if it is a medicated gum for a sore throat or other illness.

Rule:_____

Amendment:_____

_____

GA1345

Praises for a Gravedigger

Perhaps you are wondering why a person who digs graves would be praised for the job that he does. Here is an account of a gravedigger who won the praises of many.

In 1861 Elmira Camp in New York was used as a training camp for Union troops. In 1864 it was used to hold Confederate prisoners of war. Sometimes as many as 12,000 prisoners were crowded together in the camp. Very often these prisoners died of diseases and injuries sustained during the war. They were buried in Woodlawn City cemetery and two additional lots donated by the city.

John Jones, a runaway slave from Virginia, served as the caretaker. Instead of just doing his job of burying each body, he went a step further. He faithfully kept a record of the name, regiment, death date and grave number of every Confederate soldier that he buried.

In 1875 wooden markers were placed at every grave site. These were later replaced by tombstones. In addition to the individual graves, a special marker was placed for forty-nine prisoners and seventeen Union guards who were killed in a train wreck.

According to Jones' records, most of the dead soldiers came from North and South Carolina, Georgia, Alabama, Virginia and Tennessee. Many people praised John Jones, the escaped slave, who kept the records of approximately 2950 Confederates who died as prisoners of war in the Elmira prison camp in New York.

Keeper of Records

John Jones, the caretaker (gravedigger), kept such information as name, regiment, death date and grave number of every Confederate soldier that he buried.

List five ways that such information can be used.

1.

2.

3.

4.

5.

List ten jobs that require one to keep records.

1.

2.

3.

4.

5.

6.

7.

8.

9.

10.

GA1345

The Reconstruction Era

The Civil War ended on April 9, 1865, and so did 250 years of slavery for African Americans. Hundreds of Blacks had escaped to freedom, many had been freed by joining the Union Army. But all were freed when Congress passed the 13th Amendment. It forbade slavery in all states and territories of the United States. When the 13th Amendment was passed, over 3,953,000 slaves became free forever more. It would seem that African Americans now free of slavery would have an easy life, but this was not the case. Sure, they were free to do what they wanted to do and free to go where they wanted to go, but many had no place to go. Some freedmen, as they were now called, wandered about from place to place. Others were trying to find family members who were sold away from them during slavery. Still others were trying to find work to support their families. Finding work was very difficult. Many who looked for jobs found that Whites who had the money to pay them refused to hire them. With no money, no land and no place to live, what were they to do? Little had been done to prepare black ex-slaves for freedom. They needed someone or something to help them find jobs, a place to stay and a plan to get an education. Various religious and charitable organizations played important roles in helping the ex-slaves get adjusted to their new lives. Just when it seemed that all hopes of starting a new life were gone, help came. The Congress of the United States set up an organization called the Freedmen's Bureau. Now the ex-slaves could have help in getting work, wages, a place to stay and, most importantly, an education.

GA1345

Fact-O-Gon

Follow the instructions below to make a Fact-O-Gon.

1. Cut around the edge of the figure.

2. Turn over on reverse side and write an important fact about Blacks during the Reconstruction Era on each section and color each section with different colors of crayons.

Lay yarn or string here.

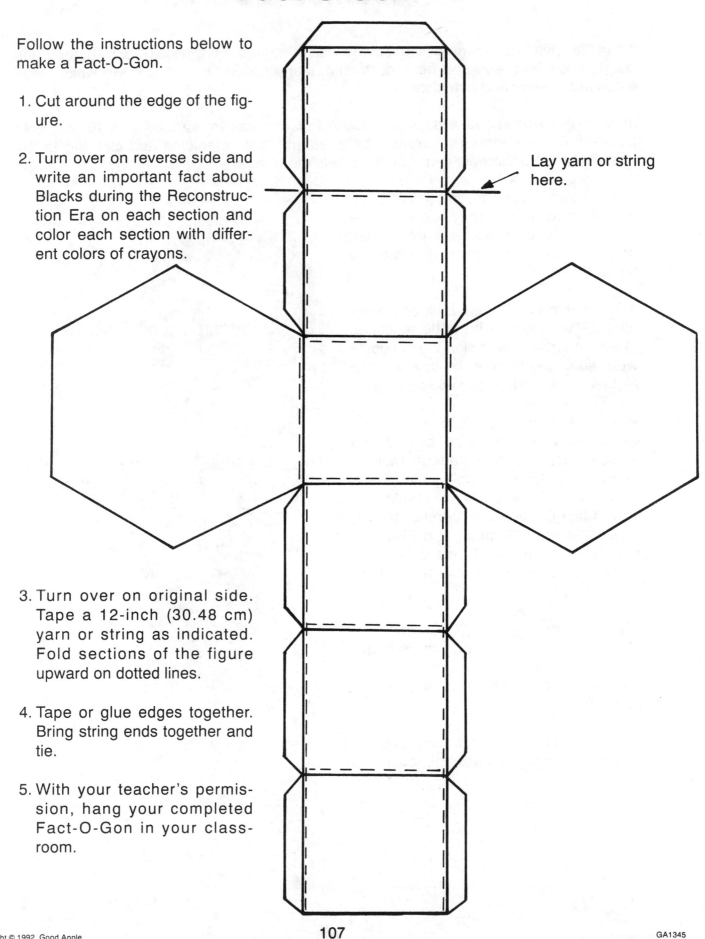

3. Turn over on original side. Tape a 12-inch (30.48 cm) yarn or string as indicated. Fold sections of the figure upward on dotted lines.

4. Tape or glue edges together. Bring string ends together and tie.

5. With your teacher's permission, hang your completed Fact-O-Gon in your classroom.

GA1345

The Freedmen's Bureau

After the Civil War, many of the South's cities lay in ruins. Fields, crops, homes and nearly everything else had been destroyed. Many people, both black and white, were wounded, hungry and homeless.

Just as the war ended a bill was passed in Congress to establish the Freedmen's Bureau. The Freedmen's Bureau was to supply food, medicine and clothing to the needy. Many Northerners came South to help the Bureau.

The Bureau helped to find jobs for ex-slaves, and it set up schools to give Blacks the opportunity to learn to read and write. Many Whites were helped by the Bureau too.

The Freedmen's Bureau built and operated 4300 schools with 9000 teachers. Over a quarter of a million black people were educated through its day schools, night schools and job training schools.

Many of today's black colleges and universities were founded during the Reconstruction Era. Talladega College in Alabama, Tougaloo College in Mississippi, Howard University in Washington, D.C., Clark College and Morehouse College in Atlanta, Georgia, and Fisk University in Nashville, Tennessee, were set up as special schools to educate black teachers.

Shaw University and St. Augustine's College both are located in Raleigh, North Carolina. Both were also founded as schools for freedmen during Reconstruction.

Today these colleges and universities have all become great institutions, offering learning opportunity for all races of people.

GA1345

College Completion

Complete the chart with information about each of the black colleges that was founded during the Reconstruction Era. Use an encyclopedia to help you.

Name of College or University	Date Founded	Location–City, State	Composition of Student Body
Example: Talladega College	1867	Talladega, Alabama	Co-educational
1. St. Augustine's College			
2. Tougaloo College			
3. Hampton University			
4. Shaw University			
5. Howard University			
6. Clark College			
7. Morehouse College			
8. Fisk University			

GA1345

Learning to Read

After the Civil War the Freedmen's Bureau organized schools in order that black ex-slaves could learn to read and write. This poem "Learning to Read" was written by a black poet named Frances E.W. Harper. It tells how anxious the freedmen were to learn to read and write. The poem was taken from her book titled *Sketches of Southern Life*, published in 1872.

Very soon the Yankee teachers
Came down and set up schools;
But oh! how the Rebs did hate it
It was agin' their rules.

Our masters always tried to hide
Book learning from our eyes;
Knowledge didn't agree with slavery
T'would make us all too wise.

But some of us would try to steal
A little from a book.
And put the words together,
And learn by hook or crook.

I remember Uncle Caldwell
Who took pot-liquir fat
And greased the pages of his book
And hid it in his hat.

And had his master ever seen
The leaves upon his head
He'd have thought them greasy papers.
But nothing to be read.

And there was Mr. Turner's Ben
Who heard the children spell,
And picked the words right up by heart
And learned to read 'em well.

Well, the northern folks kept sending
The Yankee teachers down;
And they stood right up and helped us
Though the Rebs did sneer and frown.

Poem Reading

Read the poem "Learning to Read" and answer the questions below. Then organize your class and do a choral reading.

1. What is meant by the word *Rebs*? _____

2. Why did the masters try to keep the slaves from learning to read and write?_____

   _____

3. What is meant by "learn by hook or crook"? _____

4. How did Uncle Caldwell hide his book? _____

5. What is "pot liquir"? _____

6. What would the master think when he saw the greased pages of Uncle Caldwell's

   book? _____

7. How did Mr. Turner's Ben learn to spell? _____

8. Who were the northern folks? _____

9. Who were the Yankee teachers? _____

10. What did they do? _____

GA1345

The Military Reconstruction Act

After the assassination of President Abraham Lincoln, Vice President Andrew Johnson was sworn into office. It was April 1865. Andrew Johnson, a Southerner from the state of Tennessee, was anxious to restore the Confederate states to the Union, but Congress was not so eager to do so. The Congress felt that these rebellious states should pay for their disloyalty. As president, Andrew Johnson quickly granted "home rule" to some of the states. This meant that each state could rule themselves as they saw fit. Seven months after taking office he announced, to the surprise of the Congress, that he had decided to restore all of the Confederate states. This action was angrily opposed by the Congress.

In December 1865, senators and representatives from the states that President Johnson had restored came to take their seats in Congress. Congress refused to seat them. Most of these Southerners were officers of the Confederate Army and ex-confederacy congress and cabinet members. A committee of both House and Senate members was set up to investigate and report on conditions in the former Confederate states. In June 1865, the committee made its report. It reported that the Confederate states were still too rebellious to return to the Union. The committee recommended that a constitutional amendment was needed to protect the rights of freedmen (ex-slaves).

In June 1866, Congress passed the 14th Amendment. This amendment made African Americans United States citizens. Another section of the amendment permitted Congress to reduce the representatives of any state that would not permit Blacks to vote. President Johnson's home state of Tennessee was the first Confederate state to

GA1345

ratify the 14th Amendment. But he urged the other ten Confederate states not to accept this amendment. The congressional election in November 1866 gave the control of the House to Congress.

The Congess then began to deal harshly with the southern ex-Confederate states. On March 2, 1867, Congress passed the first of the Military Reconstruction Acts. These acts went into effect at the end of the summer of 1867.

These acts required that government officials in the ex-Confederate states that were set up under Andrew Johnson be removed from office. Under the state laws Blacks could not vote, and they did not protect Blacks from being cheated, beaten and murdered.

The Military Reconstruction Acts were aimed at the ten Confederate states still out of the Union. Each of the ten states would not be restored to the Union until it completed three requirements: (1) draw up a new state constitution, (2) elect new state officials under the new constitution and (3) ratify or pass the 14th Amendment which made Blacks United States citizens.

Under the Military Reconstruction Act the ten Confederate states were divided into five military districts. Each district was headed by a Union general and four thousand soldiers to help enforce the law. It was to make sure that men, especially black men, would have the right to vote.

By June 1868, six of the ten states followed the Military Reconstruction Act and returned to the Union. By July 1870, the remaining four states had returned. As a result of the Military Reconstruction Act, 700,000 Blacks and 660,000 Whites registered and voted in the initial elections of 1867 and 1868.

GA1345

Congressional Debate

When the Civil War ended in 1865, the Confederate states had been defeated. The problem of what to do with the states that had seceded and fought against the Union had to be decided. Pretend that you and your classmates are members of the United States Congress. Discuss the pros and cons of each question below.

1. Should these states be punished for seceding from the Union? How should they be punished?

   _____
   _____
   _____
   _____
   _____

2. Who should decide the fate of the Confederate states? The Congress? The President? Both the President and Congress?

   _____
   _____
   _____
   _____
   _____

3. Should former slaves be given the right to vote?

   _____
   _____
   _____
   _____
   _____

4. Would ex-slaves be treated fairly? Should the federal government interfere in the matter?

   _____
   _____
   _____
   _____
   _____

5. Should ex-slave owners share their land with ex-slaves?

   _____
   _____
   _____
   _____
   _____

Hold a congressional debate. Make rules and vote to pass legislation on the five questions above.

GA1345

"Forty Acres and a Mule"

"Every colored man will be a slave and feel himself a slave, until he can raise his own bale of cotton and put his mark on it and say it's mine!"

These were the words of Prince Rivers, a black Army veteran of South Carolina. Before the war, slaves worked large plantations of cotton, tobacco, sugar and rice. Now as free persons they wanted to work to take care of themselves. But in order to do this they needed land of their own with crops for profit.

Thaddeus Stevens, a white congressman from Pennsylvania, had an idea. He suggested that land be taken from the planters in the states that had rebelled and left the Union. This land he thought could be given to the ex-slaves to work as their own. In this way the rebellion states would be punished and the ex-slaves would have a good chance to begin a new life and grow their own crops. Thaddeus Stevens reminded the Congress that this had been done before. The American colonists who refused to support the American Revolution were driven into Canada and their land had been taken away from them. Stevens felt that the slaves deserved the land. They were the ones who worked so hard in the fields day after day to make large profits for the landowners. The ex-slaves began to have hope that one day their dreams of owning their own land would come true. In 1862 Congress passed a law that stated that land could be seized for treason, but President Abraham Lincoln requested that the land could be taken only for the owner's lifetime. After this it would have to be returned to the owner's family after his/her death.

GA1345

On the Sea Islands near South Carolina, some plantations had been sold because the owner could not pay taxes. This land was divided into forty-acre lots and sold to freedmen for a special low price. The freedmen then started their own farms.

The land of Confederate President Jefferson Davis was taken away and given to freedmen. After two years when freedmen had begun to settle the land and farm it, the land was taken back and returned to the Davis family.

During these two years, Blacks had proved that they could be successful in working their own land.

Freedman refused to be disappointed. They still had hopes of someday having forty acres of land and a mule to work it.

Thaddeus Stevens didn't give up his fight to help the freedmen become independent farmers. His proposal was that the government would take over two hundred acres of land from ex-Confederates. The land would be auctioned off to the highest bidder. Money from the sales of the lands would be used in four ways: (1) to care for wounded veteran soldiers, (2) pay for Union war damages, (3) pay the Union war debt and (4) pay the cost of "forty acres and a mule" to each black adult male or head of a family. Again and again he urged Congress to hear his proposal, and again and again Congress refused his request.

Thaddeus Stevens died a brokenhearted man in 1868. His proposal of "forty acres and a mule" for Blacks died with him, and so did the hopes of millions of black Americans.

Your Forty

Pretend that you have been given forty acres of land represented in the space below. Make drawings showing how you would develop your forty acres. Will you build homes? Golf courses or tennis courts? Shopping centers? Parks? Stores? A shopping mall? A school? A church? Amusement parks? Other areas?

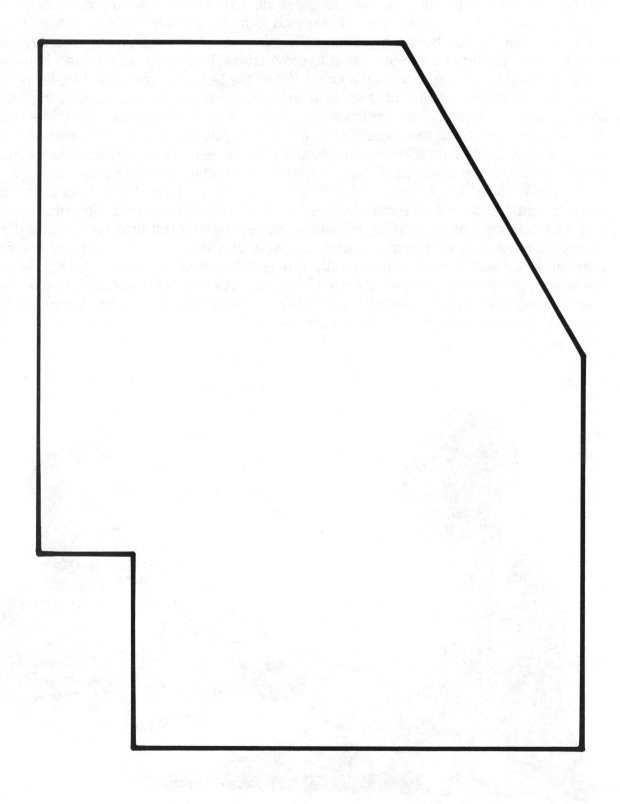

The Sharecropper

The title "The Sharecropper" could remind you of the title of a novel with romance, drama or mystery. Quite the opposite from 1868, when a sharecropper led a miserable life almost like that of a slave.

By the end of 1868, it was clear that Congress would not grant land to poor freedmen to begin a new independent life. Free Blacks had to make a living somehow. Many freedmen and poor Whites began a system of farming called sharecropping. In sharecropping each family farmed a plot of land to grow crops. The owner of the land furnished the land, seeds, farming tools and a cabin. When the tenant's crop was sold, he was to repay the landowner. Many of the freedmen who were slaves now farmed the same land as sharecroppers. The plantation land owner was in charge of selling the crops and keeping records of the unpaid debt. Many sharecroppers could not read or write. This gave the landowner a chance to cheat. In the fall when all of the crops were gathered and sold, the sharecropper was ordered to come up to the "Big House" for a settlement. For most of the sharecroppers this was a time of hope. Many hoped that the records would show that the debt for seeds and tools had been paid. Too many times this was not the case. Usually the sharecropper discovered that his crop had not brought enough money to pay his debt to the landowner. Therefore many sharecroppers remained tied to the landowner only to repeat the same situation year after year. If the sharecropper tried to leave the plantation, he would be put in jail for owing a debt. The sharecropper system was very profitable for the landowner, but for the sharecropper it was a never-ending cycle for him and his family.

GA1345

Write and Role-Play

Write a skit or play called "The Sharecropper." The scene is this:

You have been secretly learning to read and write; the landowner doesn't know that he can no longer cheat you. You have been keeping your own records.

He calls you up to the "Big House" for a settlement. His records show that you are still in debt to him after a year's work. Your records show differently.

Write the conversation between you and the landowner in the space below. When you have finished, assign parts and act out your skit.

_____

_____

_____

_____

_____

_____

_____

_____

_____

_____

_____

_____

_____

_____

_____

_____

_____

_____

GA1345

The Halls of Congress

The 15th Amendment was proposed on February 26, 1869, and approved March 30, 1870. This amendment gave Blacks who were former slaves the right to vote. It says that a voter cannot be denied the right to vote because of his race.

The southern states were forced to ratify (pass) these amendments before being admitted to the Union. Congress was not sure that these states would give Blacks the rights guaranteed by these amendments. So the South was divided into districts. A Union general with soldiers was in charge of each district. The army watched over voting and kept order.

During these years African Americans were registered to vote. For the first time in American history, black candidates were elected to positions in state and federal government. These congressmen spoke out on many issues. They were not only interested in gaining rights for Blacks but also for Indians and former Confederates who had some of their rights taken away as punishment for revolting against the Union. They spoke out for changes in election tactics and changes in education too.

The Halls of Congress

Between 1869 and 1901, twenty-two Blacks served in the United States Congress. Twenty served as congressmen and two were senators. The first Black to be seated in Congress was Jefferson Long. He was elected in 1869 from Georgia. Other congressmen, their states and terms are shown in the chart below.

Name–Representative	State	Number of Terms
John R. Lynch	Mississippi	3
Josiah T. Walls	Florida	3
John Langston	Virginia	1
Jeremiah Haralson	Alabama	1
James Rapier	Alabama	1
Benjamin S. Turner	Alabama	1
Charles Nash	Louisiana	1
James O'Hara	North Carolina	2
George White	North Carolina	2
Henry Cheatham	North Carolina	2
John S. Hyman	North Carolina	1
Richard Cain	South Carolina	3
Robert Elliot	South Carolina	3
George Murray	South Carolina	3
Robert DeLarge	South Carolina	1
Thomas Miller	South Carolina	1
Alonzo Ransier	South Carolina	1
Joseph Rainey	South Carolina	5
Robert Smalls	South Carolina	5

Name–Senator	State	Number of Terms
Hiram Revels	Mississippi	Elected to complete term of Jefferson Davis
Blanche Bruce	Mississippi	The first black man to serve a full term in the United States Senate

GA1345

The Halls of Congress

Write the name of each black congressman that served in the U.S. Congress during Reconstruction in the chairs below. Write the state that each represented beneath each chair.

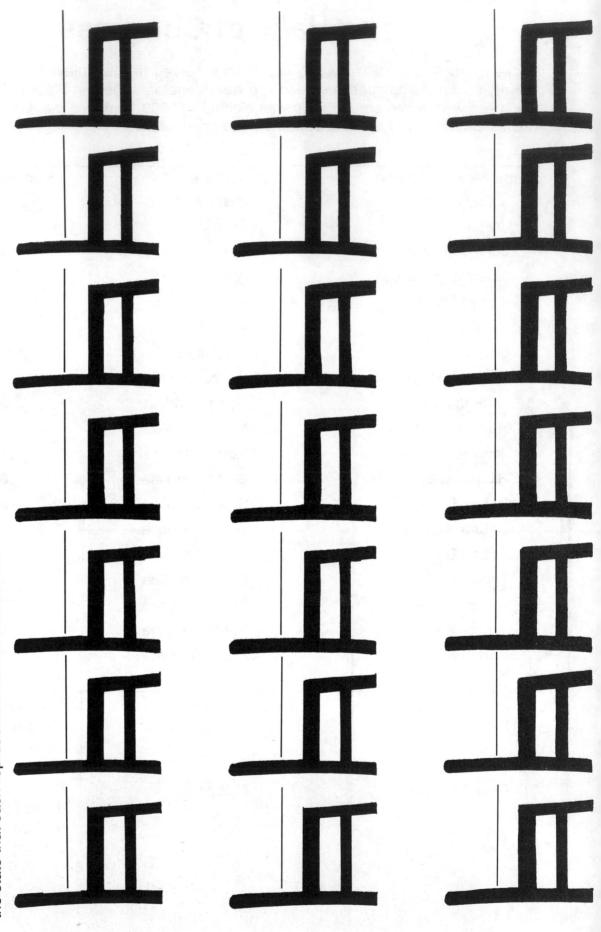

GA1345

Respond, Please...

1. Name the state that sent the most representatives to the U.S. Congress during Reconstruction._____

2. Name two things that John Hyman, Richard Cain and Robert Elliot had in common.

   a. _____

   b. _____

3. Name two black representatives that served the longest terms._____

   and _____

4. What states did they represent? _____

5. Name the two black senators that served in the U.S. Congress during Reconstruction._____ and _____

6. What states did they represent? _____

7. Name the states that sent only one representative each to Congress.

   _____, _____ and _____

8. What states were represented by James O'Hara, George White and Henry Cheatham in the U.S. Congress?_____, _____

   and _____

9. Name the black representatives from Alabama to the U.S. Congress.

   _____, _____ and _____

10. Name the black representative from Florida to the U.S. Congress.

   _____

An Opportunity

During the Reconstruction Era many African Americans became leaders in the political affairs of their states. They proved that they were as capable as anyone. All that they needed was the opportunity to serve.

Francis Cardoza received an opportunity when he was selected to become secretary of state in South Carolina in 1868 and state treasurer from 1872-1876. Cardoza was born in Charleston, South Carolina, in 1863. He attended school until he was twelve years old; then he began working to learn to become a carpenter. He worked for nine years and saved enough to continue his education. He earned a scholarship to study abroad at the University of Glascow, Scotland, for four years. At the university, he won outstanding recognition for his achievements in the Latin and Greek languages.

He also studied at Presbyterian seminaries in Edinburgh and London. After his education abroad, he returned to the U.S. in 1864 and became a minister at a Congregational Church in New Haven, Connecticut. In 1865 he was appointed head of a newly organized school in Charleston.

During the Reconstruction Era he was a member of the South Carolina Constitutional Convention of 1868. There he was elected secretary of state. Before his term ended he accepted a position of professor of Latin at Howard University in Washington, D.C. In 1872 he was elected state treasurer and was reelected in 1876. But because of home rule he was not permitted to hold this office.

Home rule meant that the states could govern themselves as they saw fit. The southern ex-Confederate states saw fit to take the voting power away from African Americans. Therefore, Blacks were no longer voted into public offices. However, in 1878 Cardoza was appointed to serve in the Treasury Department in Washington, D.C. In 1884 he became principal of a high school for Blacks in the nation's capital.

Cardoza died in 1903, but he will always be remembered as the best educated man, regardless of race, in the political affairs of his home state.

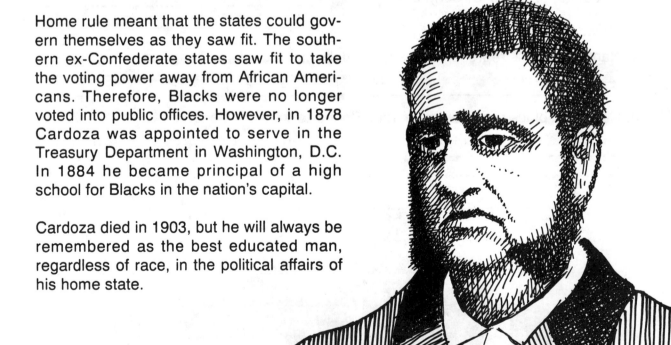

GA1345

It's Important

Francis Cardoza did not become a successful leader overnight. He had prepared himself by getting a good education.

Prepare a speech to present to your class on the topic "The Importance of a Good Education." Use the information about Francis Cardoza to help you.

Write your speech in the space below; then ask your teacher for time so that you may give your speech to the class.

_____

_____

_____

_____

_____

_____

_____

_____

_____

_____

_____

_____

_____

_____

_____

_____

_____

_____

GA1345

A Shining Example

Although several black Americans participated in government and politics during the Reconstruction Era, one person who stood out as a shining example of them all was Josiah T. Settle.

Josiah T. Settle was a Republican elector-at-large from Mississippi. He was born a slave in Mississippi. He and his family were given their freedom when the Emancipation Proclamation was signed. They settled in Hamilton, Ohio, to begin their new life. The schools were integrated there. Both white and black children attended the same school. The black children were often mistreated by both the white teachers and students.

One day, one of Josiah's white teachers found that Josiah was a bright student who learned quickly. She began to take an interest in him. She encouraged him to go to Oberlin College in 1868. In college he learned to speak well. He was chosen to represent his class in various speaking contests. After his first year in college, his money ran out and he could not continue his education. Josiah did not become discouraged. He looked for other ways to complete his education. When the Freedmen's Bureau set up a school to educate the poor and needy in Washington, D.C., Josiah enrolled there. He entered Howard University. When Howard University graduated its first students in 1927, Josiah was one of its graduates. To help pay for his schooling he worked as a clerk for the Freedmen's Bureau.

After his college graduation, he enrolled in Howard University law school. He received his law degree and passed the bar examination to practice law there. But Josiah wanted to return to his native state. He returned to Mississippi and set up a law office in Sardis. He entered politics and was nominated by the Republican Convention to serve as district attorney in the 12th judicial district.

In 1875 the Republicans lost control in Mississippi. This was not the end for this brilliant young man, however; he attended the National Convention in 1876 and 1880.

In 1883 Josiah ran as an independent for a seat in his home state (Mississippi) legislature. He defeated both the Democrat and Republican candidates. By 1885 the tide had turned against black politicians. Josiah gave up politics and moved to Memphis, Tennessee, and started his law practice there.

Within two months, he was appointed assistant attorney general of the Criminal Court of Shelby County (Tennessee). He developed a successful law practice and maintained it for several years.

Attorney at Law
Josiah T. Settle

GA1345

What If?

Suppose that Josiah had remained a slave. List ways in which his life might have been different.

_____

_____

_____

_____

_____

Was Josiah Settle a determined and bright young man? Give information from the story to support your answer.

_____

_____

_____

_____

_____

There is an organization that helps to support black colleges. It is called UNCF–United Negro College Fund. Their motto is "A mind is a terrible thing to waste." What do you think this statement means?

_____

_____

_____

_____

_____

GA1345

Loss of Rights

In 1868 General Ulysses S. Grant became president with the help of 450,000 black votes. Southerners then began to realize what Blacks could do by voting. The "Bourbons" (dissatisfied Southerners) set about to change things. First they began attacking, beating and hanging Blacks. These acts were to frighten Blacks so that they would not vote and to drive them from public office. They wanted to gain control. So they formed groups, the main one being the Ku Klux Klan (KKK). This secret organization burned homes of Blacks and beat and hanged them. It did the same for Whites who tried to help Blacks. Members of the Klan wore sheets and hoods and burned crosses as a warning. There was no protection from the Klan. Even members of the law enforcement and other county and state government officials were members.

Thousands of Blacks were murdered by the Klan, and many more were driven from their land and homes. President Ulysses S. Grant tried to bring law and order to the South, but he was unable to provide protection for the Blacks from the Klan. The terror continued to spread throughout the South. It was then that Congress decided to do something about it. In 1871 Congress passed laws to crush the Klan and other secret societies.

Hundreds of Whites were arrested, tried and convicted but the terror continued. The Republican party under which many Blacks had served in state and national government was overthrown, and the Democratic party regained strength. Year by year the Republican party grew weaker and the Democratic party used guns and other weapons to take control of elections and to frighten Blacks to keep them from voting.

In 1876 a presidential election was held. The Democrats wanted to end Reconstruction. The Republicans wanted to keep it going. When the votes were counted, both sides claimed that they had won. This was a big problem. But it had to be settled. Who would be president of the United States? To settle the issue, the Republicans promised to remove federal troops from the South. It promised that the southern states could do whatever they wanted about Blacks. The Republicans also promised to help the South rebuild their cities, farms and homes that were destroyed during the Civil War. This was just what the southern Democrats wanted. So the Democrats agreed to accept the Republican candidate, and Rutherford B. Hayes became president of the United States. When President Rutherford B. Hayes took office in March 1877, he kept his promise to the Democrats. He immediately ordered all federal troops to leave the South. The southern Democrats were now in full control. When they gained control, they made sure that Blacks would never participate in government again, at least for that time.

For a brief time after the Civil War, Blacks and Whites in the South had been governed by a government that respected both races, but now all of this was gone. Slavery was gone, but freedom had not lived long. Reconstruction with hopes and promises for better lives for black Americans had suddenly come to an end and so did the hopes and dreams of black Americans. But black Americans were not so sad. They had made some improvements that could never be taken away. They had improved their living conditions, they had the opportunity to get an education and they had sat in the legislatures of their individual states as well as in the Congress of the United States. This experience, though short as it was, could not be taken away from them.

An Organized Gang

The Ku Klux Klan is an organized gang that harasses black Americans and other minorities. The symbols of the Klan are white robes with pointed hoods and a burning cross.

Imagine that you have been appointed to organize a gang to promote friendship among people of different races. What will be the name of your gang?

Design a uniform that your gang members will wear. Write some rules for members of your gang. Design a symbol to represent your gang. Will your gang have a motto or pledge? What will your gang do to promote peace among the races?

The Great Exodus

In 1879 over fifty thousand African Americans packed up their few belongings and headed west looking for a better life. The hard days of Reconstruction, bad crops and an outbreak of yellow fever, violence and discrimination in the South had caused the great movement. The Great Exodus was led by Benjamin "Pap" Singleton. "Pap" Singleton was an ex-slave from Tennessee. He traveled throughout the South urging Blacks to follow him to Kansas. In Kansas he said Blacks could set up their own towns and communities and be free of all of the harassment that they were suffering in the South.

By the summer of 1879 ten thousand black "exodusters" had moved to Kansas. They settled there and established their own small communities.

Some African Americans did not think that the exodus was a good idea. They thought that Blacks should stay and fight for better living conditions, but thousands of Blacks continued to look for a bright future in the West. They wanted to forget Reconstruction, sharecropping, violence and discrimination. At first it seemed that they had left all these things behind. But the winter of 1879 would change their minds. The winter was very cold. Many died of diseases and starvation. They soon found that "Sunny Kansas" was not their idea of a good place to live. They soon found too that Whites had begun to settle in Kansas too. They then had to compete for jobs and land. Discrimination was a problem too. Some stuck it out but many returned to worse conditions in the South. The sudden mass migration of Blacks from the South had alarmed white southern farmers. In 1881 a senate committee was appointed to investigate this great movement. During the hearing, "Pap" Singleton testified that he was the one who started the great exodus west.

In 1882 in Topeka, Kansas, a grand celebration was given to honor Benjamin "Pap" Singleton for his part in helping Blacks to try a new life.

GA1345

Dear Diary

Imagine that you and your family were part of the great exodus west. Write on the diary page below as indicated.

Page 1: Tell of your family's reason for going west.

Page 2: Tell about the cold winter faced by you and your family in 1879.

Page 3: Write about the "Pap" Singleton grand celebration that you and your family attended in 1882 in Kansas.

Page 4: Write a diary page to a friend back home telling him that you and your family will be returning home.

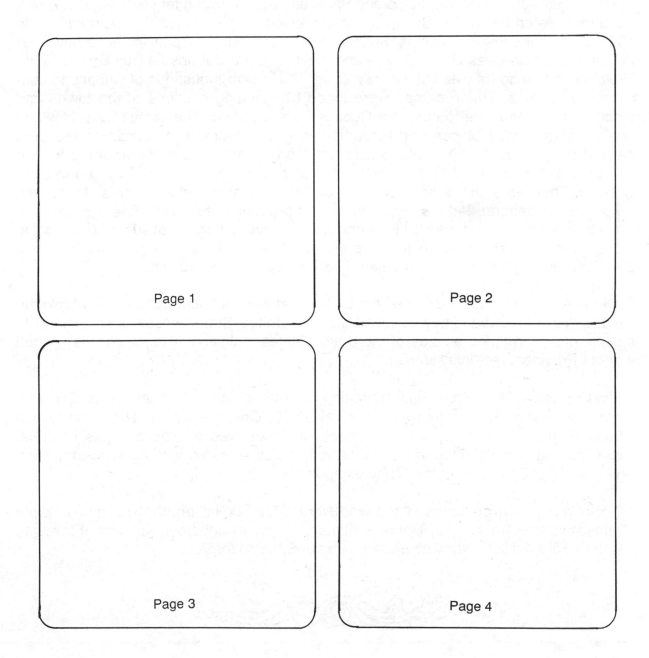

Page 1

Page 2

Page 3

Page 4

The Spanish-American War Era

On the night of February 15, 1898, a terrible explosion shattered the quiet Harbor of Havana, Cuba. It was the sound of the United States battleship *Maine* ripping apart. The explosion killed two hundred and sixty officers and enlisted men of the United States Army. Twenty-two African Americans were among the dead.

At the time of the accident no one knew for sure what caused the explosion. The explosion was investigated by both the American and Spanish governments. The Spanish government claimed that the explosion was caused by something on board the ship. But the American government felt that the explosion was caused by an underwater mine planted by the Spanish force. Whatever the cause, this incident was the beginning of a chain of events that started the Spanish-American War.

This war between the United States and Spain had been brewing for some time. 1. America had invested heavily in Cuban sugar plantations, mills, mines and railroads. 2. In 1895 the Cubans revolted against Spanish rule. 3. In 1896 the Spanish sent a new ruler to Cuba. His name was General Valeriano Weyler. To the Cubans he was known as the "Butcher," because he was such a mean ruler. 4. He sent thousands of Cubans to concentration camps. These camps were made by stringing sections of the towns and places with barbed wire to keep the Cubans from escaping. The camps were crowded and dirty. They were places of disease, suffering and death. 5. American newspapers carried the stories of this brutal treatment. Many Americans had sympathy for the Cubans. 6. African Americans were especially sympathetic toward the oppressed Cubans. They were still remembering an earlier incident in which Antonia Maceo, the black Cuban general, led his black and mulatto guerillas to attack Spanish soldiers. They burned mills and terrorized the enemy. After several periods of successful attacks, the Spanish invited Maceo to a peace talk. 7. When General Maceo arrived he was shot and killed by Spanish infantrymen. The Spanish had tricked him.

8. Many Americans had hoped that the United States would help Cuba to overthrow the Spanish ruler in Cuba. They believed that the United States should also expand to include other territories outside of the United States mainland. The Americans wanted war but President McKinley waited.

At first it seemed that Spain was loosening its hold on Cuba. 9. Then the people who were siding with the Spanish started a revolt. 10. On January 25, 1898, the United States Battleship *Maine* arrived to protect American lives and its interests in Cuba. When the battleship arrived in Havana, Cuba, it was received with courtesy. 11. Then on the night of February 15 the *Maine* exploded.

12. When the U.S. government received word of the explosion, the war cry went out "Remember the *Maine*." 13. Congress voted 89 million dollars in support of the war. 14. On April 19, 1898, war was declared on the Spanish forces.

GA1345

Chain of Action

Write an event that led to the Spanish-American War in each of the chain links. Use the numbered statements in the story to help you.

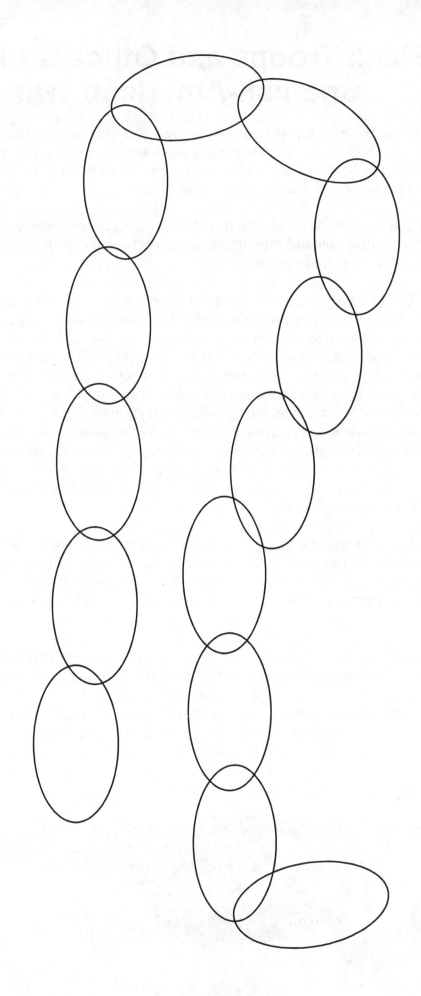

133

Black Troops and Officers in the Spanish-American War

When the Spanish-American War began in April of 1898, neither country was prepared for war. The Spanish army was strong and well armed, but they were fighting far from extra ammunition and weapons back in their home country, Spain. Their crews had not been trained properly and their supplies were short.

The United States army was not the best that it could be either. The regular army consisted of only 28,000 enlisted men scattered over the country. It would have to be reinforced by thousands of volunteers.

The United States had not been involved in a large scale war since the Civil War 1861-1865. It was handicapped by a shortage of rifles, uniforms and medicine. There was not even a transporter to carry soldiers to Cuba. When the call for volunteers went out, 182,000 men answered the call. Among the 180,000 volunteers, were thousands of black soldiers. Over sixteen black regiments of soldiers served in the Spanish-American War. All state volunteer units except those from Alabama had black officers. One infantry batallion from Ohio was led by a black major, Charles Young. Several black officers received commissions. Captain William J. Williams and Lieutenants William Herbert Jackson and George Braxton were commissioned by Governor Wolcott of Massachusetts. These three officers were part of the "L" company of the 6th Massachusetts Regiment. It later became the base of the 54th Massachusetts Infantry Volunteers who gained fame during the Civil War.

During the war Charles Young rose from 2nd lieutenant to major. John R. Lynch, a former black congressmen from Mississippi, became a major. James Young and John R. Marshall became colonels. Colonel John R. Marshall, who was the son of slaves and who studied at Hampton Institute in Virginia, was the first Black to attain the rank of colonel.

During the Spanish-American War many of the black officers met with opposition from white officers. Once a regiment of white officers refused to accept their paychecks from Major John R. Lynch, a Black. This incident was reported first to the army general, General Staton. President McKinley later approved the dispatched message. The message was that if the white troops wished to have their paychecks, they would have to receive them from Major Lynch or go without pay.

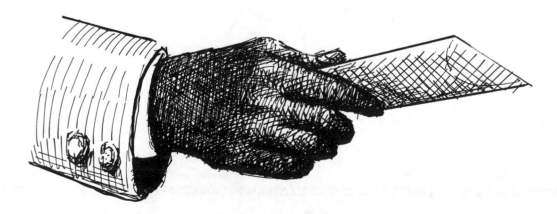

134

GA1345

Rank #1

The rank of a soldier in the United States Armed Forces is shown by patches and other insignia worn on the soldiers' uniforms. Use an encyclopedia or reference to research and illustrate the insignias for officers in the United States army.

Place the rank of each black soldier beside his name.

1. Charles Young _____

2. William J. Williams _____

3. William Herbert Jackson _____

4. George Braxton _____

5. John R. Lynch _____

6. James Long _____

7. John R. Marshall _____

Design a special medal to honor these famous black Spanish-American soldiers.

GA1345

Black Valor

When the United States declared war on Spanish forces in Cuba, black soldiers said good-bye to their families and friends and prepared themselves for battle. The 24th and 25th Infantries and the Ninth and Tenth Cavalries were among the first to be sent to Cuba. Black soldiers were treated unfairly from the very beginning. Once while the 25th Infantry (of black soldiers) was in Tampa, Florida, waiting to be transported to Cuba, other soldiers were given permission to go ashore, but black troops were not given shore leave unless they went as a group led by a white officer. The black troops were assigned to living quarters in the very bottom of the ship. These quarters were usually hot and stuffy. White troops were allowed to mingle with friends and buddies on the deck of the ship, but black troops were not permitted to have deck privileges.

These and many other unfair practices against black soldiers made army life especially difficult. Despite the odds against them, on the battlefield the black soldiers distinguished themselves time and time again. They saw action at San Juan, Las Guasimas and El Caney.

They later fought with Lieutenant Colonel Theodore Roosevelt and the First Volunteer Cavalry known as the Rough Riders. Two black units, the Ninth Cavalry and the Tenth Cavalry, gave such important support to the Rough Riders during a San Juan Hill battle that it is said without their support, the Rough Riders would have been completely wiped out. The Ninth and Tenth Cavalries showed their gallantry at San Juan Hill and brought many favorable comments about their courage.

Black soldiers fought with such valor that five of them received the Congressional Medal of Honor and one hundred were commissioned as officers during the war.

The deeds of two individual black soldiers of the Spanish-American War are listed below.

T.C. Butler: When the Spaniards were entrenched on a hill near a blockhouse, the American troops of the 24th and the 25th Infantries were growing weak. The black soldiers pushed forward. T.C. was the first man to enter the blockhouse. He took possession of the Spanish flag and delivered it to the American commander.

Elijah B. Tunnell was the first black American to die in the Spanish-American War. Tunnell was a cook aboard the United States ship *Winslow.* The *Winslow* had been disabled and was being towed away by another United States ship, the *Wilmington*. Tunnell had left his work below the deck to help fasten a towline. A shell exploded over the ship killing Tunnell and three other workers.

The Spanish-American War lasted only four months. It began in April 1898 and ended in August 1898. At the end of the war, the United States won control over Guam, Puerto Rico and the Philippines. It was an important war to win. By winning, the United States was soon recognized as a strong military power and black American soldiers had helped to make it so.

What Makes It So?

Why do you think that some groups of people treat other groups unfairly? List some reasons.

_____

_____

_____

_____

_____

Imagine that you awaken one morning to find yourself a member of another group or race. List ten or more problems that you might have.

1. _____
2. _____
3. _____
4. _____
5. _____
6. _____
7. _____
8. _____
9. _____
10. _____

You are a part of the United States Task Force for improving race relations in the United States. You are to submit your plans for better race relations to the United States. Write your plans/suggestions below. Will you ask for laws to be passed? What kind?

_____

_____

_____

_____

_____

_____

_____

_____

_____

GA1345

Charles Young
A Brave War Hero

Charles Young was born on March 12, 1864, in the small village of Mayslick, Kentucky. When he was just a youngster his parents moved to Ripley, Ohio. He finished high school there and became a teacher. In 1884 he was appointed to attend the United States Military Academy at West Point. He was the ninth African American to be appointed to the Academy, but up to 1877 none had remained to graduate. The reason was that white southern cadets made it difficult for black students entering the Academy. Many would not even speak to the black cadets, and they found many ways to harass black cadets. But Charles Young was determined to stick it out.

He performed his duty and studied very hard. When he graduated in 1889 he was commissioned a second lieutenant of an all-black unit of soldiers, the Tenth Cavalry. In 1894 he was transferred to a job as an instructor of military science at Wilberforce University, a black university in Ohio. When the Spanish-American War began in April 1898, he was appointed a major in charge of the 9th Ohio Regiment that was transferred to Cuba. It was the Ninth Cavalry and the Tenth Cavalry that showed such courageous fighting with Colonel Theodore Roosevelt and the famous Rough Riders.

After the Spanish-American War, Young served with military units in the Philippine Islands and in Haiti. In 1915 the Tenth Cavalry commanded by Young rescued Major Tompkins when they were ambushed by the Mexicans. Newspaper reports of Charles Young's leadership and bravery were widely read. Soon afterwards he was made a lieutenant colonel leading many raids into the bandit-infested desert of Mexico.

In 1917 when the United States entered World War I, Young was expected to be assigned to European service. But he was not. Charles Young and other African Americans were very disappointed. He had been a very brave and daring soldier and leader. He was the highest ranking black officer in the armed forces. Yet he was not considered for active duty. Why? Ask African Americans. Instead of assigning him to active duty, the army placed him on the list of officers to be retired. The reason given was that Young was ill. To prove the army wrong, Colonel Young rode horseback all the way from his hometown of Zenia, Ohio, to Washington, D.C., some 500 miles. Then he talked personally with Newton Baker, the Secretary of War. But Baker did not change things for him. Young then rode his horse back to Zenia and prepared himself for retirement. Then only five days before the war ended he was ordered to Grant, Illinois, to train soldiers there. When the war was over, he was sent to Monrovia, Liberia, to help organize the Liberian Army. Colonel Young wasn't just a brave and courageous soldier, he had other interests as well. He loved to write poetry and music during his spare time. He also wrote a play and then a book about Toussaint L'Ouverture, the Haitian slave who started a revolt against the French. In Zenia, Ohio, in his hometown church, Young rewrote many old hymns and serenades. He played the piano and cornet. In addition to English he also spoke three other languages well–Spanish, German and French.

In 1922 Colonel Young went from Liberia to Lagos, Nigeria, to gather material to write a book. It was there that Colonel Young contracted a fever and died. He was far away from home, but his body was returned to Arlington National Cemetery where he was buried with full military honors. A tall marble shaft marks his grave.

GA1345

Young's Ladder of Success

Place an achievement or event in the life of Charles Young on the correct dated rung on the ladder of success.

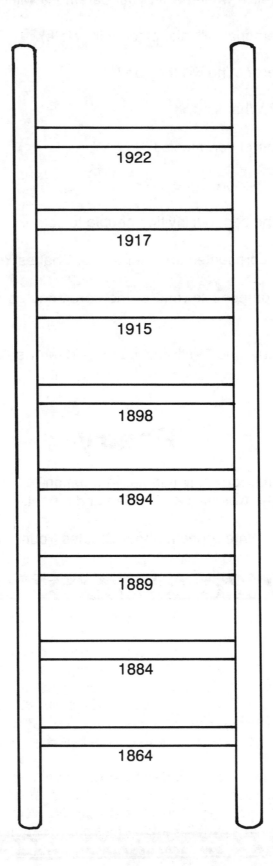

1922

1917

1915

1898

1894

1889

1884

1864

Memorial Ceremony

You have been appointed chairman of a committee to plan a memorial ceremony for Major Charles Young. Tell in writing what your ceremony will be like.

1. Decide where the memorial will take place (city, state).

2. Will you have speakers? Who will they be?

3. Will you have music? What kind?

4. Who will be the master of ceremonies?

5. Who will you invite as honored guests?

6. Design invitations to be sent out inviting people to come.

7. Design a plaque to be presented to a member of Charles Young's family.

8. Write a speech for someone to read at the ceremony as he presents the memorial plaque.

9. How will the ceremony end? Will you have a 21-gun salute? Or a lowering of the United States flag?

Poetry

Charles Young was a man of many talents. In addition to being an outstanding soldier and officer in the army, he was also a musician and a poet.

Show your poetry skills. Write a poem about Charles Young and the Spanish-American War.

The Great Migration

When the United States entered World War I in 1917, thousands of workers were taken from factory jobs in the North to fight in the war. If these factories were to continue operating, replacement workers would be needed. Factory agents toured the South. They signed up black farm laborers and other poor black Americans who were looking for a better way of life. This draining away of cheap farm labor caused great concern among the southern white farmers. They were taken by surprise when thousands of African Americans began leaving the South. Southern politicians, public officials and others tried desperately to stop the migration. But Blacks would not be stopped. They were being called north by relatives and friends who lived there. They wrote letters of hope and encouragement, urging their southern friends and family to join them in the great opportunity that awaited them. The black Southerners were more than ready to leave the South. They were tired of living in poverty. They were tired of having their children grow up without a good education. They were tired of living year after year with no improvement in their lives. So the black southern Americans packed their meager belongings and headed north to a freer, fuller life.

At first there were plenty of available jobs in the northern cities. Few African Americans had ever earned high wages that were being paid in the northern factories. Many of them moved to the northern cities for one reason only–a decent pay for a day's work. They began to vote and take part in civic affairs. Their children could go to decent schools and could even hope to go on to college. Everything went very well for a while, but soon more and more black Americans were moving North. Then it happened, as more black Americans moved north, living conditions grew worse. The black population of industry cities such as Philadelphia, New York, Pittsburgh, Chicago and Detroit doubled and even tripled in the years between 1914 and 1920. Housing became scarce. There were few places to lie. Sometimes two or three families lived crowded together in a single apartment. Housing was poor but rent was high. There were many Blacks competing for jobs. There were simply not enough to go around. If Blacks did earn enough to move to a nicer neighborhood, they found that white people banded together to keep them out. When African Americans tried to get better housing and jobs, they faced hate and prejudice from white Americans. Blacks began to be treated unfairly on the job and in stores, theaters, schools and other public places.

Black Americans were beginning to become disappointed because they were not finding the peace and freedom that they had dreamed of having. They were frustrated. During this time there were racial clashes and riots in the northern cities. Even though things had not worked out as planned, black Americans had learned quite a bit from their northern move. They had learned the importance of the vote. They had the opportunity to participate in civil and social affairs. Unfortunately, they had also learned that they were not welcomed nor accepted any place in America. But they had learned, too, that the road to equality and justice would be long and hard to travel. Most of all they had learned that there was still hope for a better and fuller life.

Choices

You are so happy today. Your mom and dad have received a letter from your Uncle Jim and Aunt Lela. They live up north. They want your family to move north too. There are eight members of your family.

> Mother–30 years old
> Father–33 years old
> You are 9 years old.
> Twin sisters–6 years old
> Brother–4 years old
> Sister–2 years old
> Brother–1 $\frac{1}{2}$ years old

There is a problem. Uncle Jim and Aunt Lela have room in their apartment for only five members of your family. Three family members will have to remain behind with your grandmother until the family finds work. It could be as long as two years. Choose the five members that you think should go first. Give your reason for each choice.

Family Member

1. _____

2. _____

3. _____

4. _____

5. _____

Reason for the Choice

1. _____

2. _____

3. _____

4. _____

5. _____

GA1345

A Letter Home

You are the father of a black family of seven children. You are looking for a job. Complete the letter below. Make your letter full of details as you tell what happened.

_____

November 10, 1921

Dear Cousin James,

    Today I went looking for a job. I walked a good ten to twelve blocks in the cold and rain. Finally I saw a sign in a window that said "Help Wanted." I went inside.

_____

_____

_____

_____

_____

_____

_____

_____

_____

_____

_____

_____

Sincerely,
Your Cousin_____

The World War I Era

When Woodrow Wilson was sworn into office in January 1913, war clouds were gathering in Europe. The next year Europe was involved in a bloody war. Many Americans had hope that the United States would remain at peace, but this was not the case. On April 6, 1917, Congress declared war on Germany. Many Americans felt that their freedom was at stake. Like all other Americans, black Americans were quick to come to the call of their country. They felt, as they had in past wars, that things would be better for them after the war. More than 400,000 black soldiers and sailors served in the armed forces in World War I.

Black soldiers fought hard to keep the freedom of the United States, but they had little freedom here for themselves. While serving in the army or navy, black soldiers met with many problems. Segregation and prejudice had followed them into the war. This was especially true in the training camps in the South. Black soldiers were often cursed, beaten and kicked around by white townspeople in the South. These people did not seem to understand that these same black soldiers whom they were mistreating were the ones who were to fight to keep America free for everyone. For the black soldier, segregation was the rule in the army, as it had been in the training camps. Over 200,000 black servicemen who were sent to Europe served in labor battalions. They loaded supplies, repaired military roads, kept military camps clean, cooked and did other humble chores necessary to keep an army going. Some units, however, were involved in combat (fighting). The 369th Infantry spent 191 days in the trenches. They fought so bravely that they were decorated by the French government with the Croix de guerre (Cross of War) award. Black soldiers participated in the battles of Argonne, Château-Thierry, Saint-Milhiel, Champagne, Vosges and Metz. The Croix de guerre was awarded to 171 black soldiers. Two of these soldiers, Henry Johnson of Albany, New York, and Needham Roberts of Trenton, New Jersey, were outstanding black heroes of the war. Both men received the distinguished French Criox de guerre award. Another black regiment, the 370th, a unit with all-black officers, was also in combat. These men fought so bravely that they were awarded sixteen Distinguished Service Crosses and seventy-five Croix de guerre awards.

Black soldiers of one other division served in the allied war effort. It was made up of the 365-368th Regiments. Only the 368th was engaged in combat duty (fighting). Five men of the 368th were awarded the Distinguished Service Cross. The whole regiment was cited by the French government for bravery.

At the end of the war, black soldiers had proven to others that they were the brave, courageous soldiers that they knew they were.

GA1345

Friendship Bowl

During World War I black soldiers suffered abuse from unfriendly white soldiers and townspeople in training camps and other areas of military life. An old saying is "In order to find a friend you must be friendly yourself." Even though the black soldiers were friendly, they were still abused. What are some other ways to make friends? Write your ingredients in the Friendship Bowl.

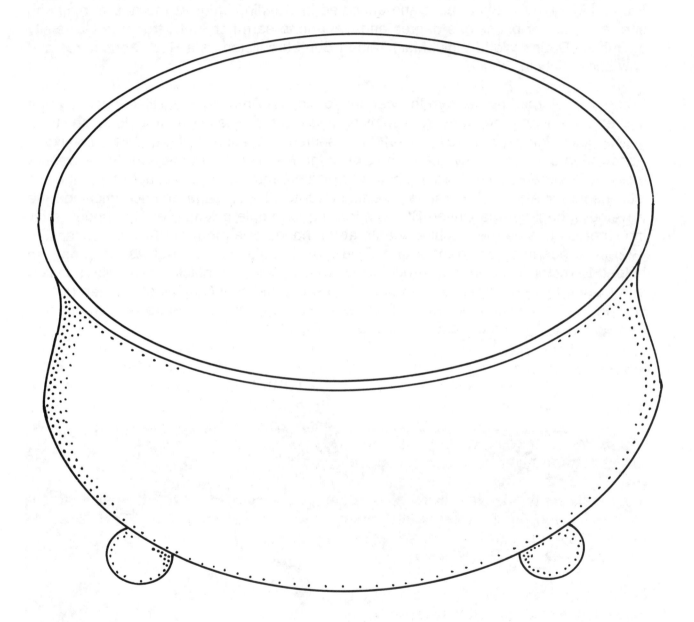

Suppose that a new boy or girl moved into your neighborhood. How would you go about making him/her your friend?

GA1345

Black Military Women

The African American women played an outstanding role in the military services of this country. During World War I black women helped in the war as members of the Red Cross, women's auxiliaries of military units and canteen war workers. One of these outstanding black World War I women was Mary Talbert Burnett. She was a patriotic worker during World War I and Red Cross nurse with the American expeditionary forces in France. Mary Talbert was born and educated in Oberlin, Ohio. At the age of nineteen she received her bachelor's degree and went on to earn her Ph.D. from the University of Buffalo. During World War I Mary Talbert Burnett enlisted as a Red Cross nurse and saw active duty in France.

When she returned home from the war she found that America was still the country that prevented African Americans from enjoying equal rights. She began to help in the struggle for black rights. From 1916 to 1920 she served as president of the Colored National Association of Women's Club and director of the National Association for the Advancement of Colored People. Through both of these organizations, she fought for first-class citizenship for African Americans. She then launched a crusade against lynching. She traveled throughout the United States speaking to people asking them to support a bill in Congress to stop the lynching (death at the hands of a mob) of black Americans. In 1922 she became president of the Frederick Douglass Memorial Association and helped to restore the home of Frederick Douglass—the great black abolitionist, speaker and leader. In 1920 she was a delegate to the International Council of Women in Norway. In 1922 she was awarded the Spingarn Medal. Afterwards she traveled throughout Europe speaking on race relations and women's rights.

Things to Do

1. Why do you think that Mary Talbert Burnett wanted to become a nurse?

2. Talk to someone who is a nurse and find out the reasons that he/she became a nurse.

3. Mary Talbert Burnett launched a crusade against lynching (an unlawful killing by a mob).

4. Ida B. Wells Barnett was another famous black American who launched a crusade against lynching. Use a reference book to write an informative paper on Ida B. Wells Barnett.

5. Write some information about the American Red Cross in the cross below. Color it red.

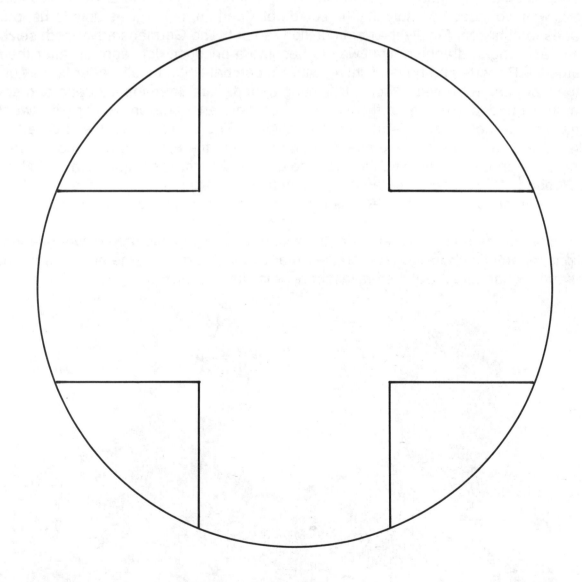

GA1345

Henry Johnson
A Gallant Black Soldier

There were over 50,000 black soldiers in the U.S. Armed Forces during World War I. But the most famous soldier was Henry Johnson of Albany, New York. Johnson was a member of the New York National Guard which became the 369th Infantry. This unit became one of the greatest fighting forces in the United States Army. The 369th Infantry was the first group of Blacks to arrive in Europe. In December 1917, they were the first Americans to cut through the German combat lines. They fought for six months without relief. They were never beaten back, and they never lost a soldier. Because of this bravery the entire unit was awarded the Croix de guerre by the French government.

Henry Johnson and Needham Roberts were the first Americans to receive individual Croix de guerre awards for unusual bravery in action. While on guard duty late one night on May 15, 1918, Johnson and Roberts fought off a German raiding party. Twenty Germans attacked the post with grenades. Both Johnson and Roberts were wounded. Roberts was wounded so badly that he could not stand up, but he was able to hand up grenades to Johnson. Finally their ammunition ran out. The Germans advanced, seized Roberts and began dragging him away to become a prisoner. Johnson ran after them. He retrieved Roberts and began fighting with his combat knife. Finally, after fierce fighting, the Germans retreated. When the fighting ended, four Germans lay dead and several more wounded. Reports of the two brave soldiers and their encounter with twenty Germans made headlines in American newspapers. The entire incident was called the Battle of Henry Johnson. For their bravery and courage, the French government awarded one of its proudest emblems the Croix de guerre to both Henry Johnson and Needham Roberts. The citation for Needham Roberts read "A good and brave soldier." The citation for Henry Johnson read "A magnificent example of courage and energy."

The citation for the entire unit read "Fought with great bravery; stormed powerful enemy positions; energetically defended; captured many machine guns, large numbers of prisoners and six cannons." But the bravest of all was Henry Johnson.

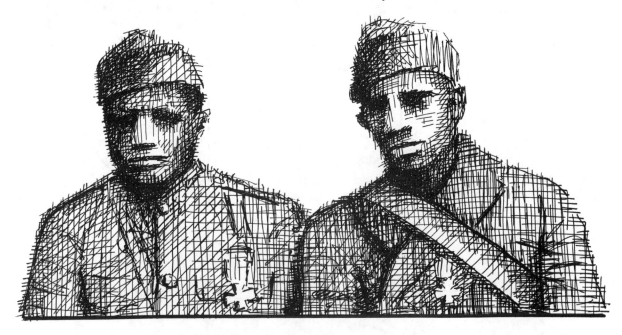

Newspaper Account

Write a newspaper account of the encounter of Henry Johnson and Needham Roberts and the twenty German soldiers. Write your information at the end of each arrow.

Name of newspaper

Headline

Date

Reporter's name

The story

GA1345

A Grand Celebration

In February 1919, a grand celebration was held along Fifth Avenue in New York City. Thousands of Americans jammed the streets. Trumpets played and flags waved. It was a celebration to welcome home the black soldiers of the 369th Infantry from World War I. The black soldiers had fought hard and brave. It was the greatest reception returning soldiers had ever gotten. The 369th deserved all of the honors that they were getting back in the United States. They had brought with them one of the best fighting records of any unit serving in World War I. They were the first American soldiers to be awarded the highest French medal for bravery—the Croix de guerre. It was given to the entire regiment for gallantry and bravery under fire. In addition many of the black soldiers earned medals for individual deeds of bravery.

As the parade continued down Fifth Avenue, people of all races cheered and waved to the brave black soldiers of the 369th Infantry. The French government had given them its highest honor, but they had not received the highest award from the United States government. During the Civil War twenty-three Blacks had won the U.S. government's highest award, the Congressional Medal of Honor. Seven black soldiers had received the Congressional Medal of Honor during the Spanish-American War in Cuba. But this highest award was not given to any black soldiers of World War I.

Black Americans were disturbed by this fact. They began to think that these soldiers were not being treated fairly. This was only one of the many disappointments that black soldiers were to face now that they were back home. Having sacrificed much for their country, black soldiers returning from the war had hoped to find a much better society in which to live. They soon realized that their hopes were false. For them and all other black Americans, things were much the same as they had been before the war.

Many states had passed "Jim Crow" laws. These laws separated Blacks and Whites in public places. These laws made black Americans second-class citizens. Black Americans could not attend movies or theaters without having to sit in upstairs areas called the balcony. Blacks could not stay in hotels or other public accommodations. They could not eat at lunch counters or be served in restaurants. Some restaurants had areas or sections in the back where Blacks could be served. Signs such as "white" and "colored" were placed over water fountains and rest rooms to separate black and white Americans. Beside the Jim Crow laws, lynching (death by mobs of white Americans) was on the increase. In the South especially, black Americans were being dragged from their homes and beaten for no other reason but because they were black.

Black soldiers had been discriminated against even as they served in the army. Now they had returned to even more of the same unfair treatments at home.

GA1345

You Design It

No black soldiers received the highest military award, the Congressional Medal of Honor, during World War I even though they were awarded the Croix de guerre, the highest French award. Now it's up to you. Design a medallion to be presented to the brave black soldiers of World War I—the 369th Infantry. Use crayons or markers to color your medallion. Then write a speech to be read as these soldiers receive their medallions.

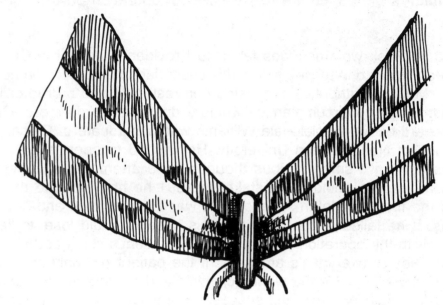

GA1345

Black Scholars and Scientists

Carter G. Woodson (1875-1950) founded the Association for the Study of Afro-American Life and History.

Percy L. Julian made pioneer discoveries in the uses of soybeans.

Daniel Hale Williams performed the first successful operation on the human heart. Here is the story.

On July 9, 1893, a black workman was taken to Provident Hospital in Chicago. The workman had been stabbed in the left side of his chest during a fight. Soon he went into a state of shock. Medical authorities suggested bed rest, cold and a drug called opium for such patients. Under no circumstances would a doctor try to do more. Open heart surgery was unheard of. Dr. Daniel Hale Williams was a graduate of Chicago Medical College, a division of Northwestern University. He wanted to operate on the patient. However, he was giving it some serious thought. If he attempted an operation and failed, his medical practice could be at stake. In 1891 he had founded the Provident Hospital. It was the first hospital in America that was founded, run and sponsored by black Americans. If he failed at the operation, his hospital could lose its license. He decided to go on with the operation. He cut open the patient's chest and sewed up the tear in the heart sac. To everyone's amazement the patient not only survived but he was soon back to work. All over the world scientists and doctors read of this amazing operation. Dr. Daniel Hale Williams had succeeded at what no other doctor had dared attempt. Throughout his medical career, Dr. Daniel H. Williams continued to make medical history. His early work in the field of medicine made possible many of the heart transplants of today.

Dr. Daniel H. Williams

GA1345

A Tough Decision

Dr. Daniel Hale Williams had to make a tough decision when he decided to perform the first open heart surgery.

Have you ever had to make a tough decision before?_____

Did everything turn out as you wanted it to?_____

Would you want to be the first to do something that has never been done before?_____

Why?_____

Why not?_____

It has been said that the human heart is the most delicate and hardworking organ in the human body. Do you believe this statement?_____

Do research on the human heart to support your answer.

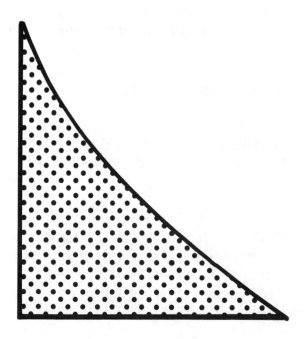 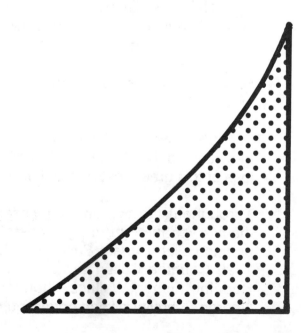

GA1345

The Harlem Renaissance

In New York City, there is a large community of black Americans. This community is called Harlem. During the late 1890's through the 1920's there was a great migration of black Americans to northern cities. During this time the population of Harlem increased from 50,000 to 80,000. Harlem then became the largest community of black Americans in the world. The Harlem Renaissance was a time during the 1920's when Blacks began to express themselves in music, art, poetry and many other fields. During this period of time, they made outstanding contributions to American culture. This Renaissance did not only take place in Harlem. Black Americans from other parts of the country began using their talents as well. However, New York was the center for the Renaissance.

In 1929 the United States entered an era called the Great Depression. It was an economic disaster. Thousands of Americans were without jobs. Factories, stores, offices and manufacturing centers were closed. When workers were laid off, there was hardly enough money for food and other necessities of life. At this time the Harlem Renaissance came to an end, but it had left its imprint on the American life. This period will always be remembered as the "Age of the Greats."

Black Writers

Langston Hughes was one of the most talented black writers of the Harlem Renaissance of the 1920's. He was born in 1902 in Joplin, Missouri, but he grew up in Kansas and Ohio. He had a lonely childhood and spent most of his time reading. When he was in elementary school, he began to write poetry.

After growing up and spending a year at Columbia University, Langston Hughes traveled as a seaman and worked wherever he could. On one of his jobs he worked in a hotel in Washington, D.C. There he met a nationally known poet named Vachel Lindsay. In 1921 when he was only nineteen years old he published his first poem. It was called "The Negro Speaks of Rivers." With the help of Vachel Lindsay he published his first book of poems in 1926. It was called *The Weary Blues*. Later Hughes went on to write novels, plays and short stories.

Langston Hughes won many awards for his contributions in the areas of poetry and literature.

In 1960 he won the Spingarn Medal for his outstanding contribution to the field of literature. Langston Hughes died in 1967 at the age of 65. The whole world mourned the loss of this great poet and writer.

Throughout the Harlem Renaissance, black American writers continued to express themselves through many forms of literature. In 1922 Claude McKay wrote a book of poems called *Harlem Shadows*. The next year Jean Toomer wrote the novel *Cane*. In 1925 Countee Cullen wrote his first book of poetry entitled *Color*. In the same year Rudolph Fisher, Wallace Thurman, Jessie Fauset, Walter White, Nella Larsen and George Schuyler all had novels published.

Student Poet

Langston Hughes enjoyed writing poetry about his people. An example is "My People." Find this poem and read it. Then write a poem about your people.

_____
(Title of your poem)

_____

_____

_____

_____

_____

_____

_____

_____

In many of his poems he gives advice to his people to encourage, uplift and strengthen them. Read Langston Hughes' poem "Dreams." Write a poem of advice to a kindergarten student.

_____
(Title of your poem)

_____

_____

_____

_____

_____

_____

_____

_____

_____

James Weldon Johnson

(1871-1938)

What do you want to be when you grow up? A teacher? A lawyer? A writer? Or perhaps a government official? Well, meet James Weldon Johnson. He grew up to be all four. He was born in Jacksonville, Florida. He was educated in Atlanta and New York. He was the first black American to pass the bar to practice law in the state of Florida. At the age of thirty, James Weldon moved to New York and began to write. Some of his most famous writings are *The Autobiography of an Ex-Colored Man* in 1912; *God's Trombones*, 1927; *Black Manhattan*, 1930; and his autobiography *Along This Way*, published in 1922. In 1934 he wrote a book about the achievements of black Americans in literature and music. It was called *Negro Americans, What Now*.

But his most famous works of all were two of his poems—"The Creation" and "Lift Every Voice and Sing." "The Creation" is still performed today by black Americans during black history celebrations. His famous poem "Lift Every Voice and Sing" was set to music by his brother J. Rosamond Johnson. This song was adopted as the national anthem of black Americans in the 1930's. Perhaps you have heard it sung at history programs and celebrations. Today, when it is played black Americans everywhere stand up and sing with sincerity and pride the words of this beautiful anthem.

James Weldon Johnson was a government official as well as a civil rights leader. From 1905-1913 he served as the united consul to Nicaragua and Venezuela. From 1920-1930, he served as executive secretary of the NAACP, a civil rights organization. He was the first black American to serve in this position.

James Weldon Johnson made many contributions to the American culture. At the time of his death in 1938, he was a professor of literature at Fisk University in Nashville, Tennessee. James Weldon Johnson continues to be remembered today. Almost every black history program includes the singing of his "Lift Every Voice and Sing," the black American national anthem.

Accomplishments

James Weldon Johnson had many accomplishments during his lifetime. Write one accomplishment in each of the newspaper squares below.

The James Weldon Johnson Times	

GA1345

Great Singers of the Harlem Renaissance

Four African Americans who excelled in music during the Harlem Renaissance were Paul Robeson, Marian Anderson, Dorothy Maynor and Roland Hayes. Roland Hayes was born in Georgia in 1897. Early in his life his mother moved to Chattanooga, Tennessee, to find work. After young Roland grew up, he worked in a foundry; then he met Arthur Calhoun, a black musician. Young Roland began taking lessons from Calhoun. He later entered Fisk University in Nashville, Tennessee, and began singing with a tour group of black American singers known as the Fisk Jubilee Singers. He studied four years at Fisk University. By 1916 he had become an outstanding singer. In 1920 Hayes went to England and sang in Buckingham Palace for King George V and Queen Mary. In 1923 he returned to Boston and gave a recital in Symphony Hall. After this performance he was known throughout America as one of the most outstanding singers in America.

Paul Robeson

Paul Robeson was born in Princeton, New Jersey, and was educated at Rutgers College. In 1923 he received his law degree from Columbia University, but he was not satisfied with a career as a lawyer. He became interested in the theater and acting. In 1925 he played the leading role in Eugene O'Neill's play *Emperor Jones*. He then began an acting concert tour throughout America and London. In 1930 he played the role of Othello at a theater in London, England. In 1940 he became disappointed with the way Blacks were treated in America and went to Russia. There he remained until the mid-1960's when he came back to the United States. In 1974 he was listed in Who's Who in America.

Dorothy Maynor

In the year of 1910, a baby girl was born in Norfolk, Virginia, to a Methodist preacher and his wife. Dorothy Maynor was that little girl's name. Like many other famous black singers and musicians, Dorothy got her early musical training in her father's church. She continued her music career to become a great soprano (singer) of international fame. In 1939 she was hired as a soloist with the Boston Symphony Orchestra. Within three months, she had sung with three leading orchestras. Dorothy Maynor had often dreamed of becoming a great singer; now her dream had come ture.

GA1345

Growing Up

When Roland Hayes grew up, he became interested in music. He met a black musician named Arthur Calhoun who helped him get a good start in becoming an outstanding singer.

The year is in the future. You have become someone famous. Tell what you have become and what famous person or persons helped you along the way.

GA1345

Survey

Paul Robeson was a lawyer first; then he changed his career and became a famous actor.

How many people do you know who have switched jobs or careers? Use the survey questions to find out. Ask five adults to answer your questions. You may ask your parents and family members. Record your information in the chart below.

Questions	Adult 1	Adult 2	Adult 3	Adult 4	Adult 5
1. What was your first job?					
2. What is your job now?					
3. How many times have you changed jobs or careers?					

*Combine your information with your classmates and make a large chart to show your results.

GA1345

I Dreamed

Dorothy Maynor had dreamed of someday becoming a great singer. This honor did not come to her overnight. It took patience, practice and hard work.

What do you dream of becoming?

_____

_____

_____

_____

What actions will you take to help make your dream come true?

_____

_____

_____

_____

Make a drawing of yourself as you are today in the first circle. Make a drawing of you as an adult in the second circle. Write your job or occupation in the space at the bottom of the circle.

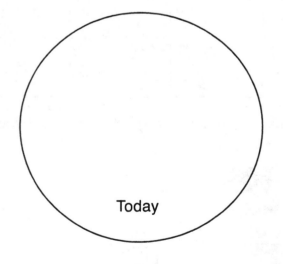

Today

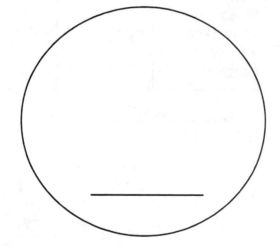

_____

GA1345

Ladies and Gentlemen, I Present...

You are the emcee for the *Sing, Sing Musical* television show to be aired on the BCC televison network.

You are to introduce your four guest singers. Write an introductory paragraph of facts about each singer on the cue cards below.

Paul Robeson

_____

_____

_____

_____

_____

_____

_____

Marian Anderson

_____

_____

_____

_____

_____

_____

_____

Roland Hayes

_____

_____

_____

_____

_____

_____

Dorothy Maynor

_____

_____

_____

_____

_____

_____

Marian Anderson

Marian Anderson was born in 1902 to poor parents in Philadelphia and began singing at the age of eight. She sang so well that people who heard her began raising money for her education. This money made it possible for her to study under a famous musician. In 1925 she was chosen from among three hundred competitors to sing with the New York Philharmonic Orchestra. She received a scholarship to study in Germany. In Berlin she was invited to tour the Scandinavian countries. During a tour of Europe she sang in Sweden, Denmark, Finland and Norway. A famous composer in Finland was so moved by her singing that he dedicated a music composition to her. She was engaged for two concerts by the London Symphony Orchestra. Of all the fame that was accorded Marian Anderson abroad, in 1939 she was denied the right to sing in Constitution Hall, Washington, D.C. When her manager tried to book her for a concert in Constitution Hall in February of 1939, an organization called the Daughters of the American Revolution protested. They did not favor a black person appearing in a concert there. People across the country were upset. Musicians, statesmen, clergyman, writers and almost everyone else denounced the DAR organization. Mrs. Franklin D. Roosevelt (Eleanor) went a step further. When she heard of the incident, she immediately resigned as a member of that organization. The Secretary of the Interior, Harold Ickes invited Miss Anderson to give her concert outside at the Lincoln Memorial. She consented to do a free concert.

On April 9, Easter Sunday morning, she sang to a crowd of 75,000 gathered at the Memorial. Another audience of several million heard her concert by radio. This concert is pictured in a mural (wall painting) decorating the walls in the new Department of the Interior building.

This incident of the DAR made Marian Anderson even more popular than she already was. Newspapers all over the country printed the story and showed the face of Marian Anderson.

Marian Anderson has made many great achievements. She has served as a delegate to the United Nations. In 1963 President Lyndon Johnson presented her the Presidential Medal of Freedom at the White House. A long list of important achievements has followed Marian Anderson all of her life. In 1961 she was named as one of the world's ten most admired women.

Marian Anderson, the greatest contralto of all times, will always be remembered by those who have heard her sing and even those who have not.

GA1345

Just Suppose

Marian Anderson was born in 1902 in Philadelphia. Her father sold coal. His income was so meager that Marian's mother, an ex-school teacher, washed and ironed for others to supplement the family income.

Just suppose that Marian Anderson had been born into a wealthy family. How might her life have been different? Write "The Marian Anderson Story."

_____

_____

_____

_____

_____

_____

_____

_____

_____

_____

_____

_____

_____

_____

_____

_____

_____

_____

GA1345

Black Music

During the Harlem Renaissance, jazz music swept the nation like a wildfire. Black musicians who came North from the South brought their music with them. Among the greatest of these jazz musicians was Louis Armstrong. Louis Armstrong was called Satchelmouth or "Satchmo" for short. He became well-known the world over as the "King of Jazz." When Louis Armstrong was a ragged little boy growing up in New Orleans, he followed the black bands through the streets as they played for parades, picnics and dances. Jazz bands also played for funerals. Louis Armstrong loved the snappy jazz music. But best of all he loved the clear, cool sound of the trumpet and the way it would shine in the sun. Louis longed to own and play the trumpet. One day a band member let him try to blow a trumpet. At first only a loud stray sound came out; then the more he tried the better he played. Some band members took an interest in Louis. He began to practice over and over again. Finally, he played well enough to march in a band. He first played with the band at picnics; then later he played with the band on a riverboat that went steaming up and down the Mississippi River. In 1922 Louis Armstrong took his trumpet and headed north for the big city–Chicago. There he played with a small band. Three years later he formed a band of his own. People liked his music. With trumpet in one hand and a white handkerchief in the other, Louis Armstrong would stroll on stage to thrill his many friends and fans with his raspy voice and his golden trumpet. His style of playing and singing has influenced jazz players all over the world. His records were bought and played by people worldwide. Anyone who grew up during those years or fifty years later knew something about "Satchmo" (Louis) Armstrong. In 1971 Louis Armstrong died at the age of 71. He was mourned by people of all ages and races. He was a legend in his own time. His music still lives in the hearts of many people the world over who knew him and loved his music.

The Harlem Renaissance was the golden age of black Broadway musicals. *Shuffle Along* was one of the best all-black Broadway musicals. The musical was written by Eubie Blake and Noble Sissle, two black talented musicians; Florence Mills sang in the musical and Josephine Baker was in the dancing chorus. Hall Johnson and William Grant Still played in the orchestra. The comedy team of Flurney Miller and Aubrey Lyles starred in the musical.

Two black American dances, the Charleston and the Black Bottom, were introduced to the world in the 1920's by black musicals. Three musical shows were *Runnin' Wild*, *Dinah* and *Hot Chocolate* with its hit song "Ain't Misbehavin'."

Charles Gilpin of Richmond, Virginia, became the first black to become a famed Broadway actor. When the great drama *Emperor Jones* opened on Broadway in 1920, Gilpin played the role of Brutus Jones for four years.

GA1345

The Golden Trumpet of Louis Armstrong

Follow the directions below to make a golden trumpet.

1. Cut out the trumpet pattern on the dotted lines.
2. Place one sheet of notebook-size paper on your desk.
3. Cover the first sheet with a second sheet of notebook-size paper.
4. Place the trumpet pattern on top of the two sheets of paper.
5. Trace around the trumpet pattern.
6. Cut along the traced lines through both sheets of paper.
7. Staple the three trumpet sheets together to make a trumpet booklet.
8. Color the top trumpet with a yellow or golden crayon.
9. Write important information about Louis "Satchmo" Armstrong on the inside trumpet sheet.
10. Turn the booklet over and decorate the back cover.

Share your booklet with a friend or hang it in your classroom.

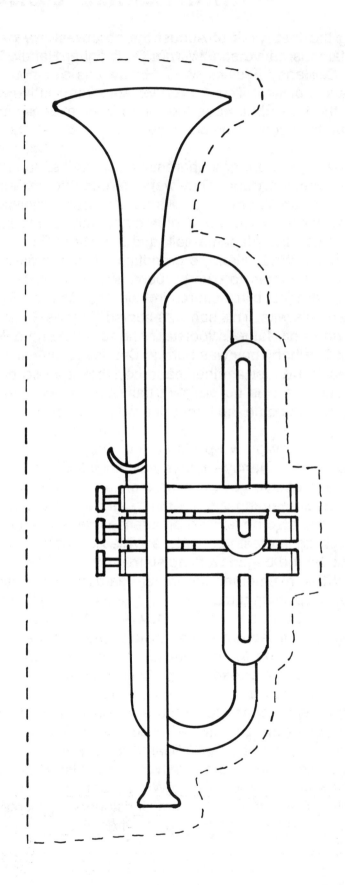

165

William Christopher Handy

During the first week of August the northwest city of Florence, Alabama, honors their most famous native son, William Christopher Handy. The week-long event is known as the W.C. Handy Festival. W.C. Handy was a famous black musician with unusual talents and abilities. This Florence, Alabama, native did not invent the form of music called the blues but made the music internationally famous. However, for W.C. Handy the road to success was not easy.

W.C. Handy's great-grandparents were James Handy and Mary Brown, two ex-slaves of Baltimore, Maryland. They were married after they obtained their freedom. His grandfather, William Wise Handy was a Methodist minister. In an attempt to escape from slavery, William Wise was captured and sold to an Alabama slave master. A Handy foot had touched the Alabama soil; and the city of Florence, Alabama, would never be the same again. W.C. Handy's grandfather William Wise settled in Florence and became the first black man to own property in the city. Later, William Wise became a minister and built the first black church in Florence. After a few years, a son was born to William Wise and his wife. This son was named Charles B. Handy. Charles Handy grew up and, following in his father's footsteps, he too became a Methodist minister. On November 16, 1873, a baby boy was born to Charles Handy and his wife. To his parents this baby seemed to be just another baby boy that they so dearly loved. But they would soon learn that this was no ordinary baby boy. Their son, William Christopher Handy, was destined to become the father of a very original form of music called the blues.

As W.C. Handy grew up his parents began to notice something about this child. He enjoyed music. Handy's father was delighted that his son was interested in music. He was sure that little W.C. would be a big help to him in his ministry. But William Christopher had something else in mind. As he grew older he became eloquent and well-learned. He also developed an intense interest in music. None of his family before had had such an interest in music as William Christopher. He was so moved by his musical interest that he began working so that he could save his money to buy a musical instrument. When his mother and father heard of his intention, they vowed never to help him succeed in playing a musical instrument and they didn't. But William Christopher continued to work and save his money. At last the day finally came when he had enough money. He hurried down Court Street, the main street of Florence. When he reached the store he was almost out of breath with excitement. The purchase was made. William Christopher had bought himself a brand-new shiny guitar. He hurried home so full of excitement to break the news to his parents. When he reached his home and revealed his purchase to his parents, they were devastated. Their dreams of their son growing up in the church and becoming a Methodist minister had turned to ashes. As they viewed the guitar that William Christopher had bought, his mother became speechless, but his father poured forth these words: "A guitar is one of the devil's playthings; take it away, I tell you." Young William Christopher was ordered out of the house and to take his guitar with him. William Christopher's parents were determined that if he wanted to go astray and live the life of the devil, as they called it, they would have no part of it.

Poor William Christopher didn't know where to turn. When his teacher at school learned that he wanted to become a musician when he grew up, the teacher wasted no time in telling him what a bad choice he was making. But finally when the time was just right, a bright ray of hope shone on William Christopher. It came through a new teacher, Y.A. Wallace. Y.A. was a young teacher from Fisk University. He had an interest in music himself, and he wanted to see his students progress in any area that they had grown to love. There and then the doors of opportunity began to open for William Christopher. Through his teacher's encouragement, young Handy began to see his talents coming into full bloom. To give his talents a chance to develop fully, William bought himself a coronet and went first to Memphis, Tennessee.

In 1902 Handy composed a campaign song for a mayoral candidate. This song later became "The Memphis Blues." In 1913 W.C. Handy established the Pace and Handy Music Company. The next year, he composed and published the famous "St. Louis Blues." The "St. Louis Blues" has been designated as the only original music art form. Closely related to spirituals, the blues is a form of music that focuses on pain, suffering and finally, joy.

In 1918 Handy moved himself and his publishing company to New York. Blues singers, musicians and composers were in great demand there. In 1928 he directed a concert at Carnegie Hall. He used black artists to portray the history and development of black music.

Handy's song "St. Louis Blues" skyrocketed him to fame. He then became the famous man that he was destined to become. W.C. Handy had been designated "The Father of the Blues."

During his lifetime W.C. Handy produced over one hundred songs. He had established a music publishing company and published over a dozen books, and he gained the admiration of people from all over the world.

When W.C. Handy died on March 28, 1958, the whole world mourned the loss of this great musician, composer, publisher and friend. William Christopher Handy will always be remembered in his hometown of Florence, Alabama. His name has been given to a place in the city called Handy Hill. An elementary school/head start building bears his name. Handy Homes, a public housing project, also bears his name. Yes, W.C. Handy has passed away but like other great men and women, he has left reminders of his brilliant abilities by the products that he has left behind.

His memory lives on, too, through the Handy. The "Handy" is a prestigious award that is given to today's best blues performers.

GA1345

Write a Skit

Using the information from the William Christopher Handy story, write a skit showing the reaction of Handy's parents when he showed them his new guitar. Ask some of your classmates to help you write and act out the skit.

_____

_____

_____

_____

_____

_____

_____

_____

_____

_____

_____

_____

_____

_____

_____

_____

_____

GA1345

The W.C. Handy Home and Museum

On a hill in the northwest Alabama city of Florence stands a two-room log cabin—the birthplace of William Christopher Handy. In 1873 when W.C. Handy was born, the cabin stood on the corner of Irvine Avenue and Beale Street. During an urban renewal project, the deteriorating home was taken apart one log at a time. The logs were numbered and stored in the basement of the W.C. Handy Elementary School.

In 1950 the Handy home was restored and a museum was opened. The restoration of the Handy home and the building of the museum was made possible by donations of Florence citizens and the Handy family. The museum contains thousands of Handy memoirs—his famous trumpet, his library, citations from famous people, his wheelchair, his many portraits, his original sheets of music and the piano on which he composed his famous "St. Louis Blues." These and other memorabilia make it one of the most complete museums of its kind in the world.

The museum is open Tuesday through Saturday from 10 a.m. until noon and from 1 p.m. until 5 p.m. On the opening day of the W.C. Handy Music Festival the home and museum form a backdrop for activities on the lawn.

On other occasions, the Cabin Committee plans special activities. The Cabin Committee is a group of Florence volunteers who devote their time to the preservation of the Handy home and the Black History Library adjoining the museum.

Handy Poster Design

Every year during the W.C. Handy Music Festival a poster is designed to announce the festival. On a piece of poster board design a winning poster for the W.C. Handy Music Festival.

GA1345

Black Organizations

When thousands of African Americans left the South to live in northern cities, they left the South to find better jobs, better homes and a better education for their children. Unfortunately these trips did not turn out as expected. Few Blacks were qualified for good jobs. Their homes were usually run-down shanties and their children attended overcrowded, run-down schools.

Black Americans needed help so they turned to two organizations: The National Association for the Advancement of Colored People and the National Urban League.

In 1910 the National Urban League was founded by a group of black Americans to find better homes and jobs. It set up agencies to help educate Blacks who had never had the opportunity to get an education in the South. It also set up recreational programs so that young black boys and girls could participate in recreation and sports.

Opportunity is the official magazine of the National Urban League. The National Urban League is still alive and active today as it continues to help black Americans find better jobs and homes.

The National Association for the Advancement of Colored People was founded in 1909 by a group of white and black Americans. The NAACP helped black Americans in a different way. It worked through the courts for justice and equality for Blacks and poor Americans. The NAACP believed that black Americans should have equal opportunities in education, jobs and politics. The NAACP publishes a magazine called *Crisis*. Over the years the NAACP has fought and won many important cases in the courts to help black Americans gain their rights. Today, the NAACP is still the leading civil rights organization as it continues to fight against injustice and inequality among black Americans and other minorities.

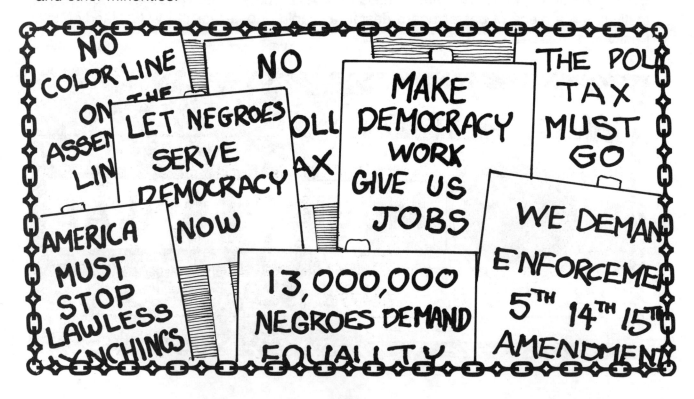

Freedom Groups

For many years, African Americans have used the group approach to help in their struggle for equality and justice. The first of these groups was the National Association for the Advancement of Colored People (NAACP) and the National Urban League (NUL). These two groups were active during the World War I Era and the years thereafter. In the years that followed, black Americans formed other groups and organizations. Listed below is information about these organizations.

Year Founded	Organization Name	Abbreviated Name	Chief Organizer
1909	National Association for the Advancement of Colored People	NAACP	W.E.B. Du Bois
1910	National Urban League	NUL	Charles S. Johnson
1915	Association for the Study of Afro-American Life and History	ASALH	Carter G. Woodson
1942	Congress of Racial Equality	CORE	James Farmer
1957	Southern Christian Leadership Conference	SCLC	Martin Luther King, Jr.
1960	Student Nonviolent Coordinating Committee	SNCC	Martin Luther King, Jr., and later Stokely Carmichael

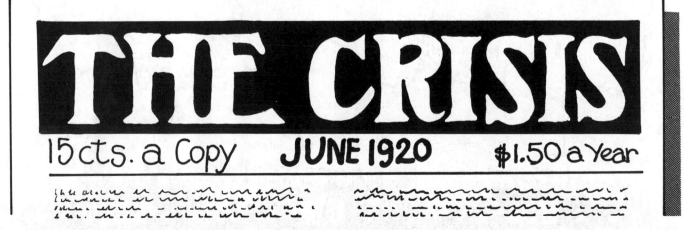

THE CRISIS

15 cts. a Copy   JUNE 1920 $1.50 a Year

GA1345

Freedom Forest

Write the abbreviated name of each African American organization in the trunk of each tree. Write the full name of the organization across the branches of each tree.

Select one of the African American organizations and write a brief report on it.

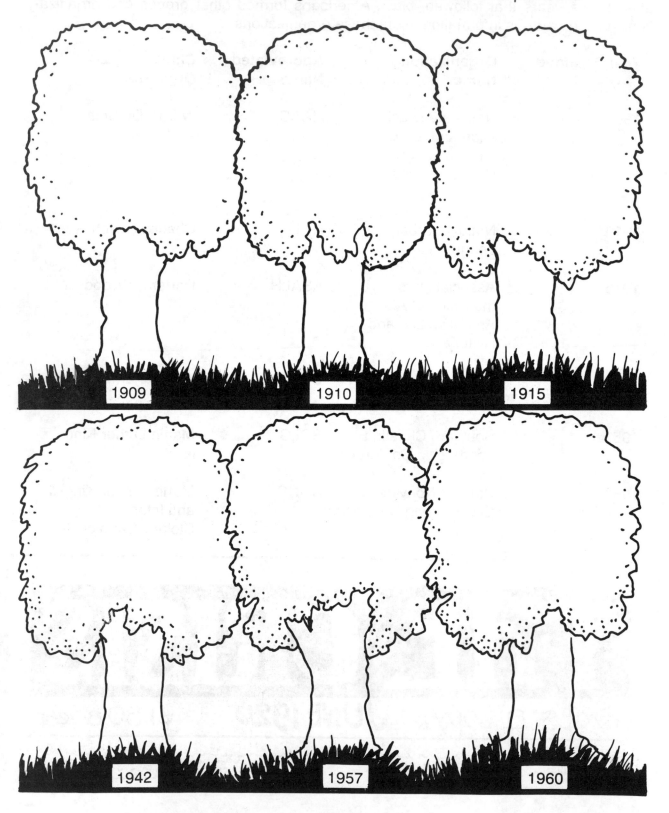

1909   1910   1915

1942   1957   1960

172

GA1345

Two Different Views

Two early educators, Booker T. Washington and W.E.B. Du Bois, became outstanding black leaders of the late 1800's and early 1900's. Both men wanted full equality for black Americans, but each proposed a different way to approach that goal.

Booker T. Washington urged Blacks to stay in the South instead of migrating to large northern cities. He wanted them to stay in the South and enroll in vocational classes to learn such practical skills as tailoring, brick masonry, carpentry, mechanics and farming. In this way he felt that black Americans could earn enough money to own their own businesses and become independent. Washington called on black Americans to focus their attention on self-improvement and money-making skills rather than protesting for equal rights. He told them to "cast down your bucket where you are." Improve yourself where you are instead of going to the North. To carry out his beliefs he organized a school in Tuskegee, Alabama, in 1881. At Tuskegee he offered courses to help black Americans develop vocational skills for financial gains and self-improvement.

William Edward Burghardt Du Bois disagreed with Booker T. Washington. He felt that black Americans could improve themselves only by fighting for their rights. He believed that the "Talented Tenth" (the brightest and most ambitious black Americans) should be the leaders for the mass of black Americans. W.E.B. Du Bois believed that only the outstanding and talented Blacks would stand up and fight for equality and justice. Instead of developing vocational skills, he insisted that Blacks should enroll in courses such as science, math, literature, languages and philosophy.

GA1345

Two Different Roads

W.E.B. Du Bois and Booker T. Washington had two different ideas about how African Americans should gain equality and justice. Write the view of each leader on the correct road.

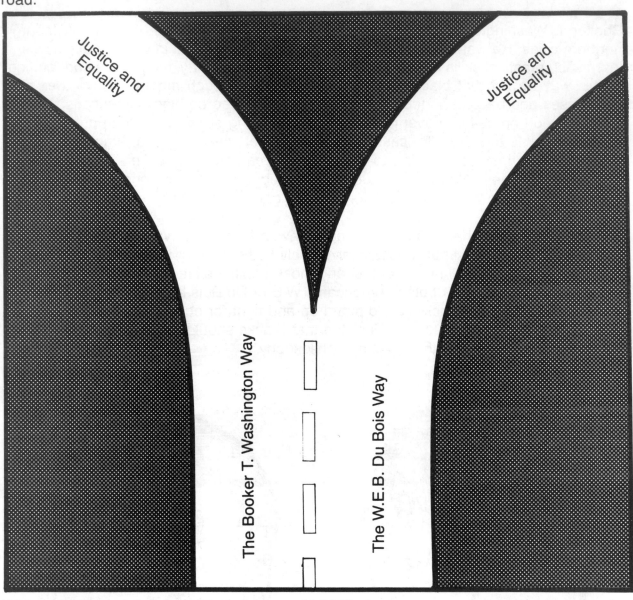

Which of the black leaders do you agree with? Why?

_____

_____

What do you think is a good way for a group of people to gain equality? Explain.

_____

_____

_____

GA1345

Outstanding Achievers in Black History

FOR
MERIT

SPINGARN MEDAL
AWARDED TO

BY THE NATIONAL
ASSOCIATION
FOR THE AD-
VANCEMENT OF
COLORED PEO-
PLE

Joel Spingarn was an American publisher. In 1913 he became a leader in the National Association for the Advancement of Colored People. While serving in this position, he thought of an idea that would reward black Americans for outstanding achievement in their fields. In 1914 he created the Spingarn Medal. The Spingarn is a gold medal that is given each year by the NAACP to a black American who has made an outstanding contribution in his or her field. Using an almanac or encyclopedia, answer the questions below.

1. In what year was the first Spingarn Medal awarded? _____

2. Who received the award? _____

3. In what year was no award given? _____

4. In 1958 the Spingarn Medal was given to ten individuals. What did they do? _____

_____

_____

5. Who received the award in 1939? _____

6. In what year did Martin Luther King, Jr., receive the award? _____

7. Who was the 1975 recipient? _____

8. How many times was the medal given in education? _____

9. List the recipient(s). _____

10. How many times has the award been given in literature? _____

11. List the recipient(s). _____

_____

12. Name the five recipients of the award in government. _____

_____

13. In 1923 the Spingarn Medal was given to a famous scientist. What was his name?

_____

14. Rosa Lee Parks received the Spingarn Medal in 1979. What did she do? Research to find out. _____

_____

15. In 1944 Charles Drew received the award in medicine. What did he do? _____

_____

16. Who was the Spingarn Medal winner in the year you were born? Research and write a paragraph of interesting information about the person.

The Great Depression

Black Thursday was the beginning of the Great Depression. On this Thursday, October 24, 1929, the stock market plunged into a steep dive. Within three weeks 30 billion dollars had been lost by investors. That was more money than World War I had cost the United States. Those who had invested their money in the stock market had suffered a great loss. It would seem that only the rich would be involved, but the Great Depression involved everyone in the United States. Even the farmers had their losses. Farm prices were at an all-time low. Then there were African Americans. Three million who had lost their jobs to machinery in the 1920's now suffered more bad times. African Americans were the hardest hit. What caused the Depression? Economists who have studied the Depression say that it was caused by several changes.

Easy credit–Too many people borrowed too much money or bought too much on credit.

Profits and dividends were too high–Businesses grew bigger and bigger and made more profits.

Machinery replaced factory workers–More goods were produced but more people were out of jobs.

Farmers were producing too many products–Extra products were not being sold.

In the factories a cycle was taking place.

1. Factories with machinery produced more goods.

2. Many people were laid off because of the machinery.

3. Without money people could not buy goods.

4. Goods piled up without being sold.

President Herbert Hoover was greatly concerned about the millions of workers who were out of jobs, and every six out of ten African Americans were unemployed. Hoover set up a national committee to help the unemployed. He thought that the poor and needy that were created by the Depression should get help from charity organizations instead of the federal government. He did not believe that the Depression would last. He had predicted that it would end in sixty days. The President was wrong; the Depression lasted much longer.

GA1345

Complete a Cycle

Fill in the blank boxes to show the cycle that occurred during the Great Depression.
Use the numbered sentences in the Great Depression information if you need help.

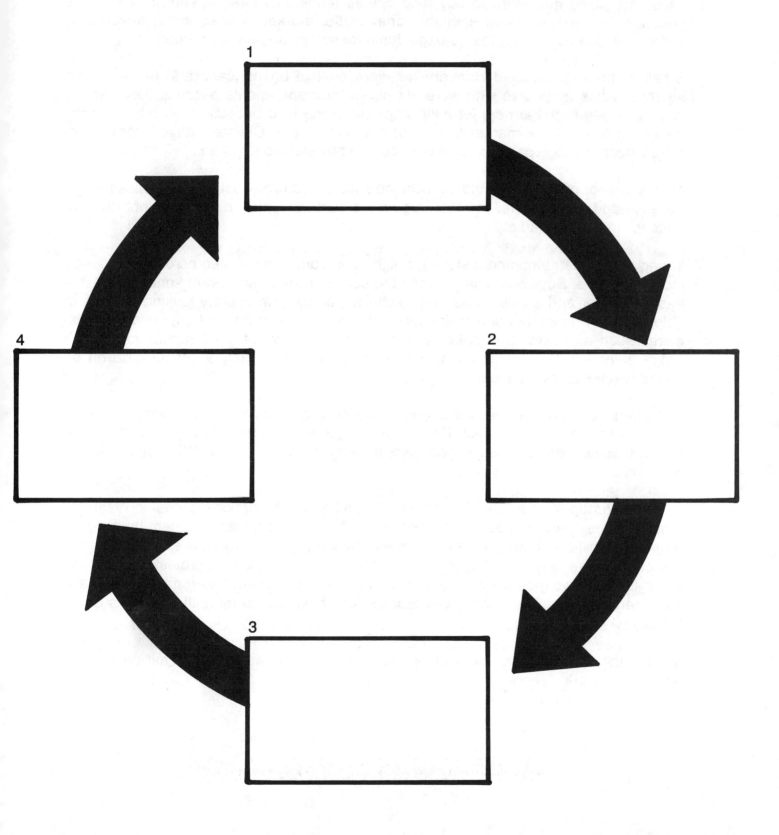

Life During the Great Depression

What was life like during the Great Depression? During this period in the history of the United States, grown men stood on street corners selling apples for a nickel to help feed their families. Bread lines and soup kitchens were set up to feed hungry Americans who could not afford to buy food. Sheep farmers in Oregon shot their animals because they did not bring enough money at the market to keep the farm running. Some men picked through the garbage dump for scraps of meat and bread.

Small communities called Hoovervilles were built of boxes, cans and tar paper on empty city lots by people who were put out of their apartments because they had no money to pay rent. Farmers let their crops rot in the field because they did not bring enough money at the market to pay for gathering them. Children stayed home from school because their parents could not afford to buy clothes for them.

On the streets of New York, old men shined shoes for a nickel. Others sold shoestrings, neckties and newspapers. In other large cities such as Chicago, people slept on park benches in the city parks.

Young boys in large numbers slept in freight train cars and traveled across the country looking for jobs. Boys and girls between the ages of sixteen and twenty-one died of diseases, hunger and exposure as they hitchhiked across the country looking for jobs to help support themselves and their families. Small children suffered from deficiency diseases such as rickets and pellagra because they could not get healthful foods with proper vitamins. Some Chicago teachers fed over 10,000 hungry school children on their already skimpy salaries.

The times were so bad that some people did not want to live. When things got really rough, people began to protest. People formed groups and marched on their city halls. In some cities, people stood in doorways to keep landlords from evicting poor families who could not afford to pay rent.

In 1932 a group of veterans of World War I marched on the nation's capital in Washington, D.C. They had not been paid a bonus that had been promised to them by the government. A bill had been passed to give veterans the bonus pay. However, because of low government funds, the bonus pay was cancelled. The veterans protested by putting up tents. After two months of waiting, President Herbert Hoover ordered troops to make the veterans leave. The troops used tear gas and bayonets to force the veterans out of the city.

In 1932 the Great Depression was as bad as it could get. More than 16 million workers were out of work.

GA1345

As the Great Depression swept the nation, millions of black Americans suffered the most. More than half of America's black population was out of work. Those who were working were not getting the full salary for their work. Black Americans in the South were even worse off than those in the northern cities. The South was the poorest part of the country. It was at the bottom in every area–health, housing, education, jobs and wages.

Cotton from large plantations was not making much money for the plantation owners. With the Depression the demand for cotton decreased. When the new synthetics, like rayon, came in, not much cotton was being used. Since there was not a demand for cotton, black sharecroppers were dismissed by white landowners. Some government help was given to white Americans, but black Americans in the South were left to starve or move north. They knew that they could not get jobs, but they could get government help in the northern cities. They had no choice. So many packed up their few belongings and began the trip north.

A New Deal

When Franklin D. Roosevelt became president on March 4, 1933, all Americans looked to him for a recovery from the Great Depression. The new president let the people know that he would help them. He did. At first he called experts from many fields to help him make the best decisions. Professors, lawyers, economists and others gave the president new ideas to help solve old problems.

The term *New Deal* was first used by Roosevelt when he accepted the democratic presidential nomination in 1932. In his acceptance speech to the American people he said, "I pledge you, I pledge myself to a new deal for the American people."

His New Deal Program was designed to pull the United States out of the Great Depression. During his term as president, Franklin Delano Roosevelt worked with the Congress to pass a series of laws to provide relief for the needy. Many changes were made in banking, business, agriculture and industries. A total of twenty-one agencies were set up to regulate these changes.

Tell It Like It Was

Tell what life was like for the following during the Great Depression Era.

1. Boys and girls between the ages of 16 and 21:

_____

_____

2. Small children:

_____

_____

3. Teachers:

_____

_____

4. World War I veterans:

_____

_____

5. Old men:

_____

_____

6. Young boys:

_____

_____

7. People in large cities such as Chicago:

_____

_____

8. Sheep farmers in Oregon:

_____

9. School children:

_____

_____

10. Farmers:

_____

_____

_____

GA1345

Leading New Deal Agencies

Date	Name of Agency	Purpose
1933	Agricultural Adjustment Administration–AAA	To increase farm income
1933	Civilian Conservation Corps–CCC	To help young men in needy families earn income working on conservation projects
1934	Federal Communications Commission–FCC	To regulate radio, telephone and telegraph systems
1933	Federal Deposit Insurance Corporation–FDIC	To insure bank deposits
1934	Federal Housing Administration–FHA	To insure loan companies against loss on home mortgage loan
1933	Public Works Administration–PWA	To create jobs through the building of schools, court-houses, bridges and dams
1935	Rural Electrification Administration–REA	To provide electricity for farm homes
1935	Social Security Board–SSB	To provide benefits for the aged, the needy, blind and disabled persons
1933	Tennessee Valley Authority–TVA	To build dams on the Tennessee River to control floods and produce electricity
1935	Works Progress Administration–WPA	To provide work for needy persons on public work projects, as well as create jobs for artists, writers, actors and musicians

Help! Help!

The letters or symbols for ten New Deal agencies are listed below. In the space provided tell what each agency did.

1. AAA _____

   _____

2. TVA _____

   _____

3. CCC _____

   _____

4. REA _____

   _____

5. PWA _____

   _____

6. WPA _____

   _____

7. SSB _____

   _____

8. FHA _____

   _____

9. FCC _____

   _____

10. FDIC _____

   _____

GA1345

Black FDR Appointees

When Franklin Delano Roosevelt became president, many outstanding black Americans were appointed to responsible government positions. **Mary McLeod Bethune**, a famous black educator, was appointed to head the division of Negro Affairs of the National Youth Administration.

William Hastie became governor of the Virgin Islands. **Robert Weaver**, an outstanding authority on housing, was the administrator of the Federal Housing and Home Finance Agency.

Walter White served as a consultant to the president. His influence with the president helped open many doors for black Americans during this era.

Ralph Bunche became acting chief of the division of dependent territories. He later won the Nobel Peace Prize in 1950 in mediating the war between the Arabs and Jews in Palestine.

Lester Walton was another black American who became a high official during the Roosevelt administration. He was appointed Minister of Liberia.

Robert Clifton Weaver served in the Department of the Interior.

Ira Reid served on the Social Security Board.

Eugene K. Jones served in the Department of Commerce.

Lawrence W. Oxley served in the Department of Labor.

Ambrose Caliver served in the Office of Education.

Edgar Brown served in the Civilian Conservation Corps.

Frank Horne served in the Housing Department.

Mary McLeod Bethune

Robert Vann served in the Justice Department. Together the Blacks serving in high government capacities were called The Black Cabinet. The Black Cabinet performed their jobs well. They pushed for economic and political equality for black Americans.

Black Americans were serving in other government positions as well. In 1933 over 50,000 black Americans were on the federal payroll. By 1938 there were well over 82,000 black government workers.

Black Americans also made gains in politics during the FDR administration. At first most black Americans voted Republican. In later years the Republican party began to disappoint black Americans because it did very little for them. Blacks began to vote democratic. In 1934 Arthur Mitchell, a black Democrat, was elected to Congress from Chicago. He had defeated Oscar de Priest, a black Republican. Adam Clayton Powell, an outstanding black minister from New York, switched from the Republican to the Democratic party.

Under the FDR administration it appeared that the doors of opportunity were now beginning to open for the nation of black Americans.

GA1345

The Black Cabinet

Write each Black Cabinet member's name in the proper office below.

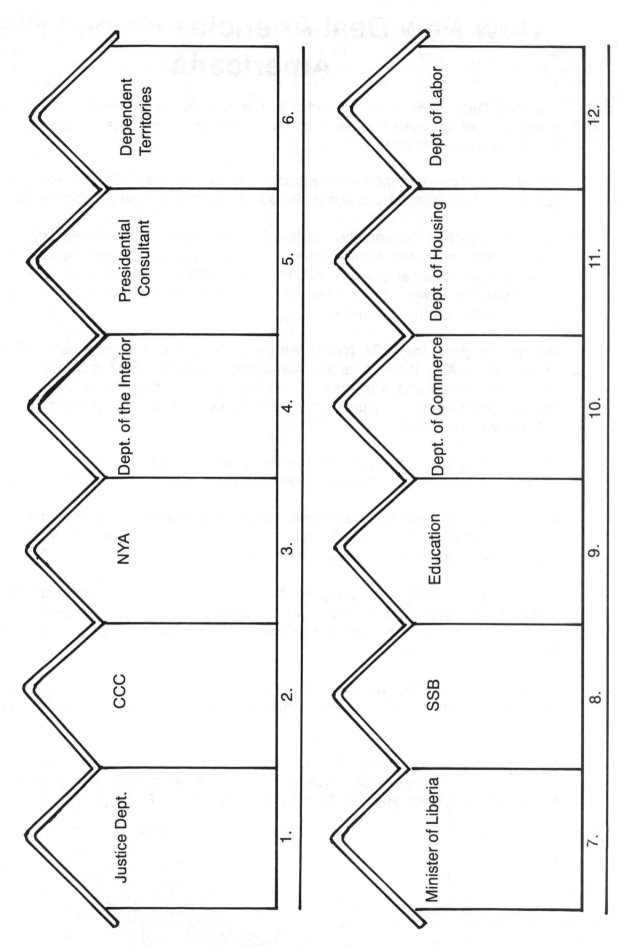

Justice Dept.	CCC	NYA	Dept. of the Interior	Presidential Consultant	Dependent Territories
1.	2.	3.	4.	5.	6.

Minister of Liberia	SSB	Education	Dept. of Commerce	Dept. of Housing	Dept. of Labor
7.	8.	9.	10.	11.	12.

185

GA1345

How New Deal Agencies Helped Black Americans

The New Deal made a big difference in the lives of black Americans. The New Deal provided relief agencies that gave advice on mother and child care, how to raise healthier babies and better diets.

Young black boys and girls were especially helped by the NYA. This was the National Youth Administration. It gave about 300,000 black boys and girls part-time jobs.

The CCC (Civilian Conservation Corps) furnished about 200,000 jobs for black boys. They worked in camps planting trees, helping to control soil erosion and conserving land and trees. The camp also taught them to read and write. Through the Public Works Administration (PWA), black Americans had jobs building schools, hospitals, playgrounds and community centers.

Another program, the WPA (Works Progress Administration), provided additional jobs for poor black Americans. This program provided jobs for black professionals and educated black Americans. Teachers, writers, artists, musicians, actors, clerks and stenographers were all put to work under this program. More than a million Blacks were helped by this program.

The AAA (Agricultural Adjustment Administration) helped to improve the life of the farmer. A few black farmers were helped by the program.

Another New Deal agency that helped thousands of Blacks buy farm land was the Farm Security Administration. The FSA made loans to small farmers. It provided the farmer with new methods of farming and marketing.

Three other programs were designed to help farmers. The Rural Electrification Administration (REA) helped provide electricity for farm homes. The Tennessee Valley Authority (TVA) built dams on the Tennessee River to control farm flooding and to provide electricity.

For black Americans who had migrated to large cities, housing was a problem. The New Deal Program built low cost, public housing and provided loans for private housing.

When Franklin D. Roosevelt died in 1945 all America mourned his passing. His New Deal programs had done so much to help black Americans. His ideas were continued by the next president, Harry S. Truman, who started the "Fair Deal" programs.

Help Symbols

Write the symbol or abbreviation for each agency that helped black Americans the most.

1. _____   Helped blind and disabled persons

2. _____   Provided jobs for black actors, writers, teachers, etc.

3. _____   Increased farm income

4. _____   Created jobs through the building of public places, schools, bridges, etc.

5. _____   Helped rural areas get electricity

6. _____   Built dams on the Tennessee River

7. _____   Provided jobs for black boys to work on conservation projects

8. _____   Gave black boys and girls part-time jobs

9. _____   Provided loans to small farmers

Black Artists

Under President Franklin D. Roosevelt's New Deal Program, black writers, actors, musicians, poets, novelists and dancers were again revived as they had been during the Harlem Renaissance of the 1920's. The WPA program provided the needed funds to support the arts. This second outburst of creativity was called the New Renaissance of the 1930's.

One outstanding black writer during this era was Richard Wright. Richard Wright was born into a family on a plantation in Mississippi. His family moved to Memphis, Tennessee. There, his father deserted his mother leaving her with two small children. The mother was not able to take care of the two small children, so they were placed in a home for orphans. By the time Richard reached high school, his mother had suffered a stroke and was paralyzed. Despite all of the hard times that Richard had experienced, he was still determined to be a writer. When he was old enough to work, he took odd jobs. He saved his money and used it to take his brother and crippled mother to Chicago. He had hoped to find a good job and a decent place to stay, but he was mistaken. The Depression had left the black Americans in Chicago struggling against poverty and hunger. Richard would not give up. He became a member of the Federal Writer's Project under the New Deal Program. In 1937 he moved to New York. There he wrote his first book, *Uncle Tom's Children*. Afterwards he produced many outstanding books. His first novel, *Native Son*, tells of a nineteen-year-old Chicago Black who accidentally commits murder and is sentenced to death. The novel condemns racial injustice. Two of his other books were *The Outsider* and *The Color Curtain*.

The great composer Duke Ellington became a famous jazz musician. He composed and wrote his first song while he was still in high school. He went on to become one of the world's greatest jazz musicians. "Mood Indigo," "Sophisticated Lady" and "Let a Song Go out of My Heart" were some of his best compositions. He later composed another great piece of music. It was called "Black, Brown and Beige."

William Dawson was a classic music composer. He composed *Negro Folk Symphony No. 1*. During the 1930's, many Black Americans became famous actors. Some of them were Richard Harrison, Ethel Waters and Paul Robeson.

Duke Ellington

GA1345

Proper Placement

Write the name of each of these black American artists under the proper heading: Ethel Walters, Richard Wright, William Dawson, Richard Harrison, Paul Robeson and Duke Ellington.

Actors   **Composers**   **Novelists**

Select one black artist from the list of names and write an information paper about him/her.

Black Athletes

Two of the most outstanding athletes during the Depression Era were Joe Louis and Jesse Owens. Both were sons of poor sharecropping families. Both were born in Alabama and both moved to the northern cities. Jesse Owens moved to Cleveland and Joe Louis moved to Detroit. Jesse Owens became a famous track star and Joe Louis became a famous heavyweight boxer.

Joe Louis was born in 1914 in Lafayette, Alabama. His family soon moved to Detroit looking for a better job and a better place to live. They were disappointed. The family barely had enough food and clothing to survive. Joe Louis attended school for a while then dropped out to work in the Ford plant. There he was assigned to heavy work. He did not mind the heavy work. He used it to develop his muscles. Then he began to box with the neighborhood boys and found that the hard work had developed his muscles so much that he could easily knock other boys down. That was the beginning of a boxing career that made him become one of the most remembered boxers in history. Joe Louis' name at birth was Joseph Louis Barrow. He later shortened it to Joe Louis. In 1934 he won his first amateur light heavyweight title. He fought his first professional fight in July 1934. He succeeded and knocked out his opponent Jack Knacken. Knacken was a heavyweight boxer. Joe Louis fought thirty-six professional fights. Then he went for the big ones! In 1937 he defeated James Braddock and became the World Champion heavyweight boxer, a title he held for twelve years, longer than any other boxer in history. Afterwards, he became known as the "Brown Bomber." During World War II, Joe Louis served in the U.S. Army. He traveled to army camps around the world putting on boxing exhibitions for army troops. He received the Legion of Merit for his record in the army.

When Joe Louis died he was buried in Arlington National Cemetery. A tall marble stone marks his grave.

Jesse Owens was the most famous runner and broad jumper in the world. In the 1936 Summer Olympic Games held in Berlin, Germany, Owens won four gold medals. He was the first athlete ever to win four gold medals at one Olympic Game. He began his track and running in high school in Cleveland. After high school graduation, he attended Ohio State University and became an even greater track star. In 1937 he received his college degree from Ohio State. The Associated Press cited him as the most outstanding track athlete of the first fifty years of the twentieth century. Jesse Owens died in 1980. In 1983 people in Jesse Owens' hometown of Oakville in Lawrence County, Alabama, decided that their famous native son should have a monument erected in his honor. Black Americans thought the monument should be placed on the Lawrence County Courthouse lawn. White citizens wanted the monument erected in a remote part of the county at Jesse Owens' homesite.

GA1345

Governor George Wallace allotted $2000 for a monument. The monument was placed at Jesse Owens' homesite. Even in its remote location, the monument was defaced and knocked over several times.

The inscription on the monument reads:

"He inspired a world enslaved in tyranny and brought hope to his fellowman. From the cotton fields of Oakville to the acclaim of the whole world he made us proud to be Lawrence countians."

Do you think that the inscription on Jesse Owens' monument really told how most people in his hometown of Lawrence County, Alabama, felt about him?

The Jesse Owens International Award is given each year to an outstanding black American track star. In 1989 Florence Griffith (Flo Jo) Joyner, a young Olympic Medal winner, was the recipient.

Who's Who?

Place the letters *J.L.* for Joe Louis and *J.O.* for Jesse Owens beside the statement that correctly describes each one. Names may be used more than once.

1. _____ He developed his muscles by doing hard work.

2. _____ He won his first amateur fight in 1934.

3. _____ He became a famous Olympic track star.

4. _____ He was a high school dropout.

5. _____ He held a college degree.

6. _____ He worked to help support his family.

7. _____ He became known as the "Brown Bomber."

8. _____ He won four gold medals at the 1936 Olympics.

9. _____ He completed high school at Cleveland, Ohio.

10. _____ He moved from Alabama to Detroit.

Listed below are twenty black American athletes. Name the sport in which each became famous. Use a reference book if you need help.

1. O.J. Simpson _____

2. Jackie Robinson _____

3. Jim Brown _____

4. Althea Gibson _____

5. Muhammad Ali _____
   (Cassius Clay)

6. Hank Aaron _____

7. Arthur Ashe _____

8. Wilt Chamberlin _____

9. Willie Mays _____

10. Sugar Ray Robinson _____

11. Florence G. Joyner _____

12. Michael Jordan _____

13. Ken Griffey, Jr._____

14. Floyd Patterson_____

15. Gale Sayers _____

16. Darryl Strawberry _____

17. Kareem Abdul-Jabbar_____

18. Joe Green_____

19. Lou Brock _____

20. Mike Tyson _____

World War II Era

When World War II broke out in 1941, black Americans were again called upon to help defend their country. Again, as in World War I, they were expected to fight for freedom abroad when they were continually being denied freedom at home.

Over two million black men and women served in the Armed Forces during World War II. At the beginning of the war, only two branches of the Armed Forces were open to black Americans. They were the Army and the Navy. In the Army, black American soldiers had to train and fight separately from white soldiers. In the Navy, black Americans could serve only as mess men. This meant that they served mostly in the preparation and serving of food.

Despite these barriers, black Americans served well, and they established a distinguished record of achievement.

Not far into the war black Americans began to protest the all-white policy of the Air Force. Yancy Williams, a black student at Howard University in Washington, D.C., threatened to bring a lawsuit against the United States Air Force unless it dropped its all-white policy and admitted black Americans.

The Air Force then opened a flight training school at Tuskegee, Alabama, to train black American airmen. Afterwards, the racial barriers were broken and black Americans began serving in the Air Force. While serving in the Air Force, black American soldiers saw more fighting than in the Navy. The 99th Pursuit Squadron was an all-black flying unit. Members of this unit served with distinction. The unit flew more than 1500 combat missions during the war. Officers and soldiers of this unit won ninety-five Distinguished Flying Crosses, one Silver Star, one Legion of Merit, fourteen Bronze Stars, 744 Air Medals and Clusters and eight Purple Hearts.

Foreign governments also awarded black American soldiers medals of bravery. Macon Johnson of South Carolina was awarded the Order of the Soviet Union. W.P. Terrell was awarded the Croix de guerre by France. Steve Rodriquez, Ernest Jenkins, George Edwards and Arthur Jackson were also awarded the Croix de guerre. William Green from Virginia won the Yugoslav Partisan Medal for Heroism. Norman Day was awarded the British Distinguished Service Medal.

In 1943 black Americans became ship captains in the Merchant Marines. They were Captain Hugh Mulzac, Adrian Richardson, John Godfrey and Clifton Fostic. They commanded a crew of both black and white American soldiers. Eighteen ships in the Merchant Marines fleet were named for famous black Americans. The *Booker T. Washington*, the *John Hope Franklin* and the *Frederick Douglass* were three of the ships named for famous black Americans.

GA1345

Another outstanding black American of World War II was Benjamin O. Davis, Jr. He organized the 332nd Fighter Group and won the Distinguished Flying Cross. Benjamin Davis, Jr., was the fourth black American to graduate from West Point Military Academy. He was the son of Benjamin O. Davis, Sr., who was the first black American to be made a general in the army. For skillfully maneuvering his fighter squadron in battle, Benjamin O. Davis, Jr., received the Legion of Merit award, the Silver Star for gallantry in combat, and the Air Medal with the four Oak Leaf Clusters. His entire unit received the Distinguished Unit Citation in 1945 from President Harry S. Truman.

Captain Charles Gandy, a division officer from Washington, D.C., was posthumously awarded the Silver Star for outstanding gallantry and leadership during an engagement "under extremely heavy fire." Another division officer Second Lieutenant Vernon J. Baker was awarded the Distinguished Service Cross for a "fighting spirit and daring leadership." Albert F. Williams distinguished himself for his soldierly qualities, leadership and dependability. For these qualities he was awarded the Legion of Merit citation.

Black Americans had served in the Coast Guard for many years. When World War II began, the Guard expanded to include three hundred black Americans who trained in seamanship, lifesaving and boat handling. One year later three thousand black Americans had joined the Coast Guard. The first black officer in the guard was Ensign Joseph Jenkins. He was commissioned in 1942.

When Black Americans returned home from the Spanish-American War, they had hoped for better treatment. When they returned from serving their country in World War I, their hopes were the same. But when they returned home from World War II, they did not hope for a better life in America. They were now ready to fight for a better life. They were not willing to accept things as they were. They were ready to change things.

Benjamin O. Davis, Sr.

Awards and Achievements of Black American Soldiers

Place the name of each soldier beside his award.

Silver Star

1. _____

_____

Distinguished Service Cross

2. _____

_____

Distinguished Flying Cross

3. _____

_____

Legion of Merit

4. _____

_____

Distinguished Service Order (Great Britain)

5. _____

_____

Airman's Medal

6. _____

_____

Croix de guerre (France)

7. _____

_____

_____

_____

_____

GA1345

A World War II Hero
Dorie Miller (to the Rescue)

It was early Sunday morning, December 7, 1941, when Dorie Miller, a young black Navy cook, was preparing the breakfast meal for soldiers aboard the USS *West Virginia*. Many of the soldiers had been at parties the night before and were sleeping late. The dining hall was almost empty. Suddenly a loud explosion rang out, then another. Almost immediately the loud speaker blasted the message "Air Raid! Air Raid!" Without warning, the Japanese had made a surprise attack on Pearl Harbor, the United States naval base located near Hawaii in the Pacific Ocean. Alarm bells rang out throughout the ship. By now all soldiers were headed for the deck of the ship. When Dorie Miller reached the deck, he discovered the ship's captain lying in a pool of blood, his stomach torn apart by a torpedo blast. Dorie lifted the captain up and carried him to a safe spot. One soldier called to Dorie to help pass ammunition to two machine gunners on the front deck. But Japanese torpedoes were falling so fast that before Dorie could help, one of the gunners was struck down. Dorie went to the unmanned machine gun. He was not trained to operate the machine gun. In those days black Americans were only trained to be cooks and stewards in the Armed Services. Without training, Dorie Miller began firing the machine gun. He aimed the gun and blasted away at the Japanese planes. He is credited with bringing down four Japanese bombers without himself being injured. Because of this brave act, Dorie Miller was awarded the Navy Cross. This medal was established in 1919 and is awarded for exceptional heroism in combat.

Admiral Chester Nimitz, Commander-in-Chief of the Pacific Fleet, pinned the ribbon medallion on this tall, black hero and read this citation: "distinguished devotion to duty, extraordinary courage and disregard for his own personal safety during the attack on Pearl Harbor." Dorie Miller, the son of a sharecropper from Waco, Texas, was only twenty-two years old when he received his citation.

In December of 1943, two years later, Dorie Miller was killed in action in the South Pacific. But his memory lives on as a man of great courage and determination. Every year the Dorie Memorial Foundation of Chicago holds a memorial service in his honor, and in New York a group of houses bears the name of this courageous brave man, an early hero of World War II.

The Daily Reader

You are a rerporter for *The Daily Reader* newspaper. Write your report on the Dorie Miller story by completing the news form below.

Who was the hero? _____

What did he do? _____

When did he do it (date)? _____

Where did the event take place? _____

Doing More

List the names of the sixteen United States military medals and decorations. One is listed for you.

1. ___Purple Heart_____

9. _____

2. _____

10. _____

3. _____

11. _____

4. _____

12. _____

5. _____

13. _____

6. _____

14. _____

7. _____

15. _____

8. _____

16. _____

On the back of this sheet, draw a picture of the Navy Cross. Write Dorie Miller's name beneath the drawing. Write the words of the citation that were read when he received the Navy Cross.

The Plan—a March on Washington

Perhaps you have heard of the 1963 "March on Washington" in which Dr. Martin Luther King, Jr., led over a quarter of a million people to protest unfair treatment of African Americans in voting, housing, jobs and other areas. That was an important march, but it was not the first time that a march on Washington had been planned. This is the story of the first planned march on Washington by a large group of African Americans. When the Japanese bombed Pearl Harbor on December 7, 1941, America began to prepare itself for war. Industries needed more and more workers to produce war materials. African Americans made some gains in employment, but they were not getting their fair share of the war industry jobs. Time after time, Blacks were turned down when they applied for these jobs. "Is it fair?" they asked themselves. "While our black soldiers go away to fight in the war, shouldn't we have some of the jobs that produce materials for the war?" Black Americans knew the answers to these questions, and they decided that something should be done to call attention to these unfair job practices. Week after week black American newspapers wrote of the country's failure to give Blacks their fair share of war industry jobs.

In 1940 the leaders of two black American organizations, the NAACP and the Urban League along with A. Phillip Randolph met with Mrs. Franklin Roosevelt. They asked first that the armed forces be integrated so that black soldiers could have the same rights as other soldiers. They also asked that provisions be made so that African Americans could get their fair share of war industry jobs. After the meeting a few changes took place, but Black Americans felt that they were not enough. When President Roosevelt heard of A. Phillip Randolph's plan to march on Washington, he was afraid that such a large demonstration would embarrass America in the eyes of other nations. So, he agreed to order an end to discrimination in war industry jobs, but A. Phillip Randolph and other black American leaders wanted an end to discrimination in government jobs as well.

Finally, when the planned march was only one week away, President Roosevelt issued Executive Order 8802. It stated that "There shall be no discrimination in the employment of workers in defense industries or government because of race, creed, color or national origin." A. Phillip Randolph went on national radio (there were no televisions) and told African Americans the news. The planned march on Washington had been called off, and a victory celebration would be held in its place. The door of opportunity had been opened. Thousands of Blacks went to work in aircraft plants, shipyards and ammunition factories. The executive order had not ended discrimination in the armed forces. This would come later, but it had ended discrimination in the war industries and government jobs. This taught black Americans an important lesson—to stand together and speak with one voice.

Let's Organize

The word *organize* means "to arrange or put in order." Listed below are ten ideas from "The Plan—a March on Washington." Organize the ideas in the order in which they appear in the story.

_____ Black Americans had learned to stand together and speak with one voice.

_____ The Japanese bombed Pearl Harbor.

_____ In 1940 the leaders of two black American organizations and A. Phillip Randolph met with Mrs. Franklin Roosevelt.

_____ Americans began to prepare for war.

_____ A. Phillip Randolph had an idea—to organize a march in Washington, D.C.

_____ Week after week black American newspapers wrote of the country's failure to give Blacks their fair share of war industry jobs.

_____ Finally President Roosevelt issued Executive Order 8802.

_____ Time after time Blacks were turned down when they applied for war industry jobs.

_____ "There shall be no discrimination in the employment of workers in defense industries or government because of race, creed, color or national origin."

_____ A. Phillip Randolph went on national radio and told African Americans the news.

GA1345

Protest

A protest march is a group of people who march in the streets. They usually carry signs on placards to express their beliefs about something. Listed below are several topics that some people have special feelings about. Select two of the topics and express your beliefs about them on the signs below.

The Homeless	Civil Rights	Endangered Species
Child Abuse	War	Drugs
Pollution	Peace	Drunk Drivers
The Environment	Nuclear Energy	Honest Politicians
Wildlife	Whales	Better Schools

You may add other topics if you like.

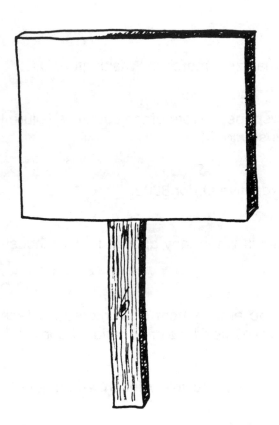 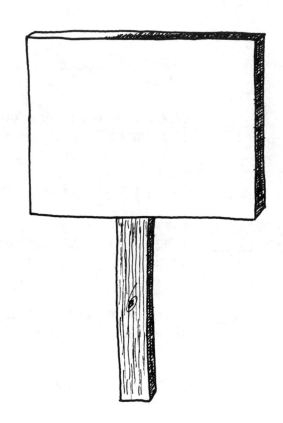

Most protest marches have a leader. Think about the type of person needed to lead a protest march. List six characteristics that you think such a leader might have. Would you be a good person to lead a protest march? Why or why not?

_____

_____

_____

Planning

There is a saying that "If you fail to plan, you plan to fail." What do you think this saying means? Write your explanation in the space below.

_____

_____

_____

_____

_____

Make a list of all of the different and unusual things that people plan for. Be creative. Try to think of things that no one else will think of. Use the back of the page if you need to.

Example:

1. ____wedding_____

2. _____

3. _____

4. _____

5. _____

6. _____

7. _____

8. _____

9. _____

10. _____

A Black Four-Star General

On February 11, 1920, the youngest of seventeen children was born to Daniel and Lillie James who lived in Pensacola, Florida. The child's name was Daniel James, Jr. His mother and father were very intelligent people. They wanted the best education for their child. When his mother found that he was not getting a proper education, she opened a school and taught him herself through the seventh grade.

His mother taught him many important lessons of life. She taught him to work to get ahead. "Don't give up and never turn your back on God, your country or your flag," she said.

Daniel lived near the U.S. Naval Aviation in Pensacola. He was fascinated by the navy trainers who flew the sky near his home. When he was twelve years old he got a job at the airport so that he could pay for flying lessons. He wanted to fly for the navy but the navy did not permit African Americans to become pilots. Still "Chappie," as he was called by his family, did not give up. When he finished high school, he went to Tuskegee Institute (University) and got a college degree in 1942. He remained at Tuskegee as a flight instructor in the Army Air Force Aviation Cadet Program. He graduated number one in his class and became a second lieutenant.

During 1943-48 Lieutenant James was actively involved in protests for equal rights of African Americans in the military. In 1948 President Truman ordered the Armed Forces integrated. Now both black and white Americans would train together. In 1950 James and another pilot had a plane accident. When the plane crash landed, the pilot was knocked out. James himself was locked in, but he managed to free himself and rescue the unconscious pilot. James was burned severely and was hospitalized with a back ailment. For quick thinking and action in rescuing the unconscious pilot, he was awarded the Distinguished Service Medal.

In Korea he was awarded the Distinguished Flying Cross for flying difficult combat missions. After six months in Korea he was promoted to captain. While serving in Vietnam, he flew seventy-eight combat missions. When he came home, President Johnson gave him a hero's welcome.

Time after time Daniel "Chappie" James, Jr., proved himself a brave and patriotic soldier. Quickly he was promoted colonel, then brigadier general and lieutenant general. On September 1, 1975, General "Chappie" James, Jr., became the first Black in history to rise to a full general status. He was now a four-star general.

"Chappie" had followed his mother's good advice, and he had become a success. On February 1, 1978, after serving in the U.S. military for thirty-five years, "Chappie" retired. Twenty-four days later on February 25, he died of a heart attack.

GA1345

Opinion

1. What important things did "Chappie" James' mother teach him?

   _____

   _____

   _____

2. What do you think caused "Chappie" to become interested in flying?

   _____

   _____

   _____

3. At the age of twelve "Chappie" had a job at the airport. Do you think that he was too young to work?

   _____

   _____

   _____

4. Use an atlas or reference book to find the state in which Tuskegee University is located.

   _____

5. General James was a great patriotic speaker. What do you think *patriotic* means? Use a dictionary to check your answer.

   _____

   _____

   _____

6. In one of General James' speeches, he said that everyone should know the words to the national anthem, "Star-Spangled Banner." Do you know the words? Write the words to the first verse in the space below. Use reference books if you need help.

   _____

   _____

   _____

   _____

   _____

   _____

   _____

   _____

James' Things

Listed below are twenty-five words associated with General Daniel "Chappie" James, Jr.

Can you find each word?

```
V H T Z U T U S K E G E E M E J Y Y R L W
E W K N E O T P V K N Z A P H H T K M G C
Y T F A E G U D S S A V T T Q L E C W L F
C X C H W G A O Q N I P N Q P X Q J Y T A
C H B Q L W I J A O R I A I D P O I F T A
E B Y M X E N L B S P H N O P J Y C H M D
O K V F M L W Z L S O T E O Z P X G J S A
M C C E L R P X Q E R W T N E D I C C A Z
H C K O F I F W J L T E U D B L R L E A E
N K M S L K S S X U U N E R F D U O O Y V
A E E D J O T R E C N O I T A C U D E T L
S M D P J R N J S A Q G L C F J O E V Y M
R A A U X O E E Y R A T I L I M I M Z K U
V V L R I O R N L D D Z U T S A H I B P N
H F T S G A A V I A T I O N N N F W L A I
B V S E M O P E A A D V I C E T Y V V D T
W I R U D O R A R L R G G N U E Z Y A T I
M T J A O A G P R O F T L G N I D M G M G
Z Z B P D X C J D X K F T R M V Z E T C L
```

intelligent	airport	education	combat	colonel
Tuskegee	flight	aviation	pilot	lessons
accident	medal	mission	brigadier	advice
parents	navy	program	military	Korea
Vietnam	lieutenant	rescue	trainer	cadet

From Janitor to Admiral

At the beginning of World War II, black Americans were not permitted to participate in the general services of the navy. They were employed only in such areas as food preparation and service. They could not become naval fighters or be educated in the skilled trades of the navy. But in 1942, all of this changed. The Secretary of the Navy announced that black Americans would be accepted as volunteers in the general services of the navy. In 1942 a black American named Samuel L. Gravely enlisted in the United States Naval Reserve. His naval duty was to clean up the pool hall. Gravely had joined the navy to do more. He wanted to attend the navy training schools and to become an important person in the navy.

Samuel Gravely was born on June 4, 1922, in Richmond, Virginia. He grew fond of pigeons and raised them in his backyard. He attended Armstrong High School in Richmond and went on to Virginia Union University. He graduated in 1948. While he was making personal changes in his life, the navy was making changes too. In 1944 an order was issued. It stated that employment in the navy would be based on individual performance, not race as it had been in the past. The navy then opened the Robert Small Naval Training Camp, Great Lakes Naval Training Base in Illinois and another one in Hampton, Virginia, to prepare black Americans for training in many skilled trades. One of the students to attend the Great Lakes Training Camp was Samuel Gravely, Jr. After completing his training at Great Lakes, he reported to Hampton, Virginia. He was then assigned to the V-12 unit at UCLA. He later attended the pre-midshipmen school in New Jersey. In August 1944, he was appointed to the position of midshipmen at Columbia University in New York City. In December 1944, he graduated. He became the first black American to have done this. After his graduation he was commissioned an ensign. This was the turning point in his navy career. His climb to success had begun. First he received submarine training and was assigned to the submarine chaser the *US SPS 1264* where he served as communication officer, electronics officer and later as executive and personnel officer. His later assignments and training included:

1949—Recruitment officer at the Naval Recruitment Station, Washington, D.C.

1951-1952—Attended naval postgraduate school in Monterey, California

Radio officer aboard the battleship USS *Iowa*

1953—Communication officer on the cruiser ship the USS *Toledo*

1955—Security officer at the Third Naval District in New York

1957—Training in amphibious warfare, Coronado, California; operation officer on the ship USS *Seminole*

1959-1960—Executive officer on the destroyer the USS *Theodore Chandler*

1961—Commanding officer of the USS *Theodore Chandler*

GA1345

1962–Commander of the USS *Dalgout*, becoming the first black American ever to command a United States warship

1963-1964–Trained in naval warfare at naval college in Newport, Rhode Island

National emergency program manager, Arlington, Virginia

1966-1968–Commander of the destroyer the USS *Taussig*

1970–Commander of the warship the USS *Jovett*, one of the navy's most modern guided-missile ships

1971–While commanding the *Jovette* off the coast of Vietnam, he received notice that he and astronaut Alan Shepherd had been selected from among 2000 other candidates for promotion to rear admiral.

Admiral Samuel Gravely was overjoyed. He had become the first black American to be assigned to a naval college. He had become the first black American to command a U.S. warship, and now he had become the first black American to become rear admiral. When he speaks of his success he says, "A guy who really wants to work and do a good job can be a success anywhere."

In 1980 Admiral Gravely retired from active duty in the navy and returned to his next love, raising pigeons and chickens. According to reporter Richette Haywood in the December 1990 issue of *Ebony* magazine, Admiral Gravely now serves as Senior Corporate Advisor for Potomac Systems Engineering. Admiral Samuel Gravely, Jr., now lives in Haymarket, Virginia, where he raises pigeons and chickens on his two-acre rural estate. At the age of 68, he still remains one of the most respected military consultants in the nation.

GA1345

Admiral

Admiral Samuel Gravely, Jr., believed that anyone who really wants to work and do a great job can be a success anywhere. Do you believe this? Explain your answer.

_____

_____

_____

_____

What advice can you give to a person who wants to be successful in life?

_____

_____

_____

_____

Before Admiral Gravely became successful in an area, he was trained and educated in that area. When you grow up, what job do you want to be successful in?

_____

_____

_____

_____

Find out about the necessary training and education that will be necessary for your success in this particular job.

_____

_____

_____

In order to be successful, Admiral Gravely had to move to different locations during his career life. Would you want to do this? Why? Why not?

_____

_____

_____

List some advantages of moving from one location to another.

_____

_____

_____

List some disadvantages.

_____

_____

_____

GA1345

Famous Firsts

During and after World War II, African Americans began to make some progress in their fight for equality and justice. Several became the first of their race to be appointed to government positions. Others were first to advance in sports, literature, opera and other fields.

1947–Jackie Robinson became the first Black to play major league baseball.

1950–Gwendolyn Brooks was the first Black to win a Pulitzer Prize.

1950–Ralph Bunche won the Nobel Peace Prize. He was the first black American to do so.

1955–Marian Anderson became the first Black to sing a leading role in the Metropolitan Opera in New York.

1957–Althea Gibson became the first Black to play national indoor tennis. She was also tennis champion at Wimbledon.

1960–Wilma Randolph became the first Black to win three Olympic gold medals in track and field.

1963–Sidney Poitier became the first black American to win an Oscar for best actor in the movie *Lilies of the Field.*

1966–Andrew Brimmer became the first African American to serve on the Federal Reserve Board. This board regulates the nation's central banking system.

1966–Constance Motley became the first black woman to be appointed judge of a Federal District Court.

1966–Edward Brooke became the first black American to be elected to a federal office as U.S. senator from Massachusetts.

1966–Robert C. Weaver became the first black American cabinet member as Secretary of Housing and Urban Development.

1967–Thurgood Marshall became the first black Supreme Court Justice.

1969–Shirley Chisholm became the first black congresswoman.

1977–Andrew Young became the first black ambassador to the United Nations.

1977–Patricia Harris became the first black woman cabinet member, Secretary to the Department of Housing and Urban Development.

GA1345

Information Chest

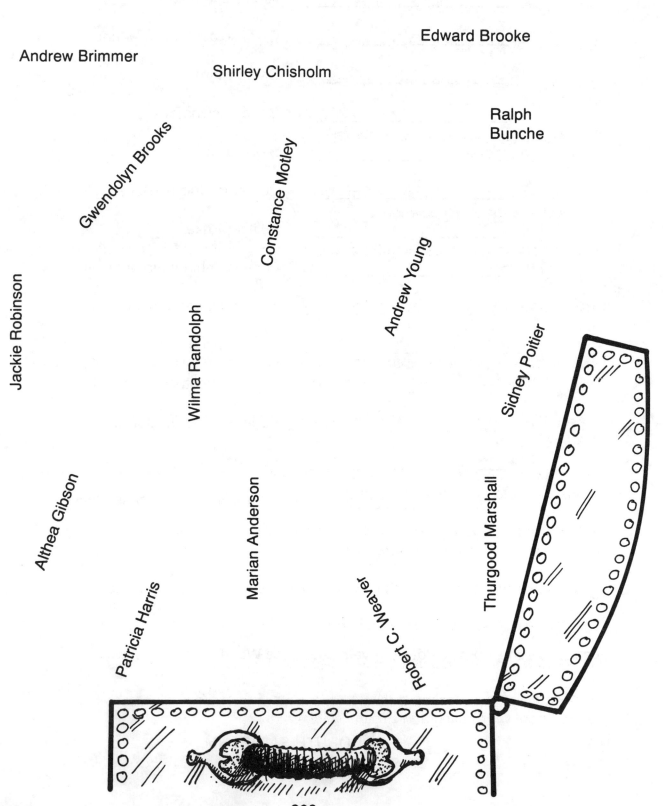

Edward Brooke

Andrew Brimmer

Shirley Chisholm

Ralph Bunche

Gwendolyn Brooks

Constance Motley

Jackie Robinson

Andrew Young

Wilma Randolph

Sidney Poitier

Althea Gibson

Marian Anderson

Thurgood Marshall

Patricia Harris

Robert C. Weaver

First Matches

Select the correct name from the Information Chest on page 209 and write it next to the correct "first."

1. _____ Metropolitan Opera

2. _____ Tennis champion

3. _____ Olympic gold medal winner

4. _____ Oscar winner

5. _____ Congresswoman

6. _____ Baseball player

7. _____ Supreme Court Justice

8. _____ Pulitzer Prize

9. _____ Female cabinet member

10. _____ Male cabinet member

11. _____ Nobel Peace Prize

12. _____ Massachusetts senator

13. _____ Federal Reserve Board

14. _____ Woman judge

15. _____ United Nations ambassador

Unscramble the words below to reveal one of the World War II firsts.

GODORUTH SALARLHM

GA1345

Black Scientists and Doctors

During the World War II Era, there was a tremendous growth in the number of professional black Americans. Doctors, lawyers, teachers, social workers, ministers and research scientists were using their skills to make America a better place to live.

On a dark night in 1950, an exhausted driver fell asleep at the wheel of his car and crashed, badly injuring himself. The accident happened in North Carolina. The man was rushed to a local hospital. He was badly in need of a blood transfusion, but the local hospital was designated "for whites only." This man was a black American and the hospital turned him away. The man bled to death. He was only forty-five years old. The man who was turned away was the famous black American Dr. Charles Richard Drew. Dr. Drew developed a process of changing blood into plasma so that it could be processed and preserved. He organized the American Red Cross blood banks. During World War II he organized a blood collecting service that saved thousands of soldiers' lives. But the hospital had turned him away and he had lost his life. When he died the whole world was stunned. Dr. Drew is an excellent example of a great American who worked for the betterment of all mankind. His blood collecting techniques are still being used today.

Percy Julian was a famous research chemist. He invented drugs to treat the eye disease called glaucoma. He also experimented and developed an inexpensive way to make cortisone. Cortisone is an important drug used to treat inflammation such as arthritis. In 1913 he studied in Vienna and received his Ph.D. degree there. He later headed the Chemistry Department at Howard University in Washington, D.C. In addition to this, Dr. Julian made many helpful products from soybeans. He owns the patent (right) to more than one hundred chemical products. He later opened his own research laboratory. It was called the Julian Research Institute. One of his patents was for a firefighting solution from soybeans. This solution saved many lives during World War II.

Dr. Charles R. Drew

GA1345

Lifesavers

Both Dr. Charles Drew and Dr. Percy Julian helped save lives during World War II. Beneath each name, tell what important things they discovered.

Dr. Charles Drew	Dr. Percy Julian

Do you think that the local hospital in North Carolina was responsible for Dr. Drew's death? Give reasons for your answer.

_____

_____

_____

_____

_____

_____

_____

Garrett Morgan was another Black American "lifesaving" scientist. Use reference books to find out about his lifesaving inventions.

_____

_____

_____

_____

_____

_____

_____

Black American Writers

During the early years of World War II and the years that followed, black American novelists, playwrights and poets put forth their best efforts and produced some of their best literary works.

One of the most versatile writers of this time period was Langston Hughes. He wrote poems, plays and novels. His play *Mulatto* ran on Broadway for more than a year. Richard Wright a bright writer of this era, wrote two outstanding novels, *Native Son* in 1940 and *Black Boy* in 1945. Both of his books were chosen for excellence by national book clubs. In 1946 novelist Frank Yerby wrote *The Foxes of Harrow*. His book made the best-seller list. It was the first novel written by a black American to make the best-seller list. William Motley's novel *Knock on Any Door* was the story of an Italian boy growing up in an American city.

One of the greatest of the Post World War II novels was written by Ralph Ellison in 1952. It was entitled *Invisible Man*. It told about black American life in the United States. It earned him the National Book Award. That same year, James Baldwin wrote his first novel, *Go Tell It on the Mountain*. It told of Baldwin's life in Harlem during the 1930's. In 1961 Baldwin became a literary figure of the civil rights movement when he published his second novel, *Nobody Knows My Name*. His next novel, *The Fire Next Time,* was a prediction of the racial unrest that was to come in the mid 1960's.

In 1950 Gwendolyn Brooks became the first black American to win a Pulitzer Prize. Her prize-winning volume of poetry was called *Annie Allen.* Ann Petry became well-known when she published her first novel called *Streets*. It is the story of a mother struggling to raise her son in the slums of New York City.

In 1959 playwright Lorraine Hansberry wrote her Broadway hit play *A Raisin in the Sun*. The play was the story of a black American family's struggle to get out of a Chicago ghetto. In the early 1960's LeRoi Jones (Imamu Amiri Baraka) won praises for his work called *Dutchman*.

In 1968 Eldridge Cleaver wrote *Soul on Ice*. It was a written record of his life in prison. Nikki Giovanni was a leading black American poet. *Black Judgment* was one of her exceptional collections of poetry. It was published in 1970. That same year, Charles Gordone won the Pulitzer Prize in drama with *No Place to Be Somebody*. In 1976 Alex Haley wrote *Roots*. In *Roots* he traced his ancestors and family tree back two hundred years to Africa. *Roots* won him the Pulitzer Prize. Novelist Chester Hines died in 1984 but not before his novel *Cotton Comes to Harlem* became a major motion picture.

Alice Walker's novel *The Color Purple* also became a major motion picture in the 1980's. In 1987 August Wilson won the Pulitzer Prize for his play called *Fences*. In 1988 Toni Morrison won the Pulitzer Prize for his novel *Beloved*. Today, black American writers continue to add outstanding works to the expanding field of literature.

GA1345

Whose Pen?

Write the correct author's name in each blank. Authors' names may be used more than once. Place an asterisk (*) beside the five Pulitzer Prize winners' names.

1. _____ Native Son

2. _____ No Place to Be Somebody

3. _____ Annie Allen

4. _____ Beloved

5. _____ Cotton Comes to Harlem

6. _____ The Foxes of Harrow

7. _____ Streets

8. _____ Knock on Any Door

9. _____ Nobody Knows My Name

10. _____ Invisible Man

11. _____ Soul on Ice

12. _____ Roots

13. _____ A Raisin in the Sun

14. _____ The Color Purple

15. _____ Fences

16. _____ Black Judgment

17. _____ Mulatto

18. _____ Black Boy

19. _____ Go Tell It on the Mountain

20. _____ Dutchman

GA1345

Black American Performers and Entertainers After World War II

In 1969 black American James Earl Jones won the Broadway Tony award for best stage actor for his portrayal of boxer Jack Johnson in the drama *The Great White Hope*.

In 1970 Cleavon Little won the Tony for best actor in a musical. He played the role Purlie in *Purlie Victorious*, written by black American actor and playwright Ossie Davis.

In 1966 and 1967 Bill Cosby won the Emmy award as television's best male actor, for his role in the TV series *I Spy*. In the 1980's and 1990's Bill Cosby produced and starred in one of the nation's best-loved television programs, *The Cosby Show*.

In 1968 Diahann Carroll starred in *Julia*, a television comedy about an attractive widow and her son.

In 1970 *The Flip Wilson Show* became a nationwide hit. It featured the famous comedian Flip Wilson playing the role of a "sassy" female called Geraldine.

Other leaders in the entertainment world were blues singer Ray Charles, crooner Nat "King" Cole; country music singer Charley Pride; soul singers Aretha Franklin and James Brown; gospel singer Mahalia Jackson; jazz musicians Louis Armstrong, Miles Davis and Erroll Gardner. Famous singing groups were the Mills Brothers, the Temptations, the Ink Spots, the Platters, the Jackson Five and the Supremes. The leader of the Supremes, Diana Ross, has since left the Supremes and has become a major singing star. In the same manner, Michael Jackson of the Jackson Five left his group and became a singing sensation. His album *Thriller* with his top-selling record "Beat It" was a thriller. It won the 1983 Grammy award. Another singing group, the 5th Dimension, won the 1967 Grammy award for their record "Up, Up and Away."

Other Grammy award winners included Roberta Flack in 1972 with her song "The First Time Ever I Saw Your Face" and 1973 "Killing Me Softly with His Song"; 1973 Stevie Wonder for his album *Innervisions*. He also won Grammys in 1974 and 1976. In 1984 black American singers Tina Turner and Lionel Richie were both Grammy award winners.

Notable movies of the year (August 1988 to July 1990) included these famous black American actors and actresses: Whoopi Goldberg starring in *Clara's Heart*; Morgan Freeman starring in *Clean and Sober*; Ossie Davis and Ruby Dee starring in *Do the Right Thing*; James Earl Jones starring in *Field of Dreams* and *Lean on Me*; Richard Pryor starring in *See No Evil, Hear No Evil*; and the movie *Tap* starring Sammy Davis, Jr.

Today's black Americans continue their success as they star in television, movies and Broadway productions.

GA1345

List Them

Make a list of some of the most recent black American performers that you know. Give the area of performance or entertainment.

Name	**Area of Entertainment**
Example: Arsenio Hall	Television

Name	Area of Entertainment
_____	_____
_____	_____
_____	_____
_____	_____
_____	_____
_____	_____
_____	_____
_____	_____
_____	_____
_____	_____
_____	_____
_____	_____
_____	_____
_____	_____
_____	_____
_____	_____

GA1345

The Civil Rights Era

During the Civil Rights Era of the 1950's and 1960's, three main areas were the focus points for black American rights: housing, education and voting.

Housing

Many cities in the United States had laws that forced black and white Americans to live in separate communities. These laws were called housing codes. Under the housing codes a black American family could not buy a house in a neighborhood that was all white. In 1917 a Supreme Court case ruled that these laws violated the 14th Amendment and therefore these laws were unlawful. Still, many neighborhoods continued to be segregated because white American families signed an agreement called a covenant in which they promised not to sell to black Americans. In 1948 these agreements were ruled unlawful. But open housing still remained a problem. Many real estate agencies refused to show, sell or rent houses in white neighborhoods to black Americans. In the years following World War II, many Blacks moved to the northern cities. They could not live where there was good housing, so many crammed into already crowded slum areas. In 1962 President John F. Kennedy issued an executive order that housing built with federal project money could not discriminate in renting to black Americans. In 1963 over 200,000 black and white Americans took part in a march on Washington, D.C., to call the nation's attention to many problems such as job, housing, voting and education that were causing problems for millions of African Americans.

President Lyndon B. Johnson signed into law a new Civil Rights Act. This act forbade discrimination by race in selling and renting houses or apartments. Many black Americans then had the opportunity to move to a better neighborhood. But this was not the end of the housing problem. Many black Americans who could afford to move into better neighborhoods were harrassed by white Americans. Many black Americans suffered violent attacks against them when they moved into "white" neighborhoods. Some had their new homes burned or bombed by angry white Americans. Even today in the 1990's some white Americans have not changed their negative attitudes toward black Americans.

Education

In 1896 the Supreme Court ruled that it was lawful for black and white Americans to attend different schools if the schools were equal. For years American schools remained separate, but they were not equal. While white Americans attended classes in up-to-date buildings, black Americans attended classes in run-down buildings (dilapidated) or meeting halls or churches converted to classrooms. This kind of inequality grew worse as the years went by and black Americans continued to attend school in inferior and inadequate facilities. There was also inequality in the area of teachers' salaries. White American teachers were paid more than black American teachers. The Supreme Court decision of "separate, but equal" was not working. American schools were separate, but they were far from equal. In 1933 the black American organization, the NAACP, provided lawyers to go to court to win the right of black Americans to attend tax-supported colleges and universities. The next year they went to court again. This time they wanted equal salaries for black American teachers.

Large organizations such as the General Education Board, the Rosenwald Foundation, the Phelps-Stokes Fund and the Ford Foundation have spent large amounts of money to help make black American schools equal. But black Americans and their white friends were beginning to think that as long as American schools were separate they would never be equal. In 1954 a team of black NAACP American lawyers led by the brilliant Thurgood Marshall went to court. In May of that year the Supreme Court ruled that separate schools were unlawful. It stated that black Americans could now attend the best schools of white Americans. Black Americans were very happy about the Supreme Court decision. Now their children could have the same opportunity to get a good education as any one else in America.

For a time, life seemed brighter. A heavy burden seemed to have been lifted from the shoulders of Blacks everywhere. But things were not so much better after all. In 1955 individual states were to submit a plan for desegrating their schools so that black Americans and white Americans could attend the same schools. Federal Courts would review the plans and decide if they were lawful. In some places school officials obeyed the Supreme Court order and began immediately to make plans to integrate their schools. But southern states did not want to obey the Supreme Court decision. Some school systems went so far as to close down their entire school systems because they did not want black and white Americans to go to school together. Throughout the South organizations and other groups organized to resist desegregation. In 1959 when black American high school students in Little Rock, Arkansas, tried to attend Central High School, violence broke out. Orval Faubus used the National Guard to prevent further violence; and to protect the black American students from white mobs, President Dwight D. Eisenhower sent federal troops to Little Rock. The Supreme Court decision had been made but southern states kept refusing to obey the orders. In the 1960's civil rights laws were passed. These laws required that schools that did not follow the desegregation order would have their federal funds cut off.

During the years that followed much more progress was made in the area of inequality in education.

Voting

Another area in which black Americans were being treated unfairly was that of voting rights. Blacks had been granted the right to vote by the 15th Amendment, which was passed on March 30, 1870. At the end of the Reconstruction Era, however, laws were passed in many states requiring poll taxes and literacy tests in order to keep black Americans from voting. Those who did qualify to vote were often threatened and harrassed. As a result, they could not participate in the government in their cities or towns. Therefore, they could not help to change things for themselves. Many black Americans felt that the time had come. For too long they had been second-class citizens. It was time for them to try to make things better for themselves and their children.

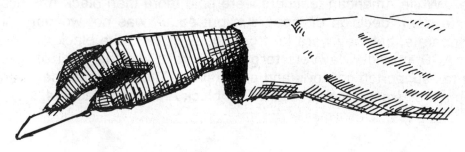

GA1345

In January 1965 Dr. Martin Luther King, Jr., began a voting rights campaign in Selma, Alabama. Civil rights workers went door to door to get Blacks to vote. They were often beaten and bullied. Dr. Martin Luther King, Jr., planned a march to the state capital of Montgomery to inform Governor Wallace about the unfair treatment of black American voters. Governor Wallace banned the march, but Dr. King and other civil rights workers were determined to carry out their plan. On March 7, 1965, five hundred marchers set out on the march from Selma to Montgomery. The Selma police used tear gas, nightsticks and whips to break up the march. Many marchers were beaten and injured. Newspapers and televisions carried accounts of the inhumane treatment of black Americans in the South. Hundreds of people both black and white Americans rushed to Selma in support of the marchers. Over 2500 people joined the march. When state troopers blocked their paths, the marchers turned away peacefully. President Lyndon Johnson then asked Congress for a bill to protect black American voters. He also announced that he would send federal troops to Selma to protect the marchers so that they could complete their march to Montgomery over seventy-five miles away. Black Americans waited; finally Congress acted. In August, Congress passed the 1965 Voting Rights Act. The 1965 Voting Rights Act removed all remaining barriers so that black Americans could have the right to vote. This act was extended in 1970 and again in 1975. After the passage of the 1965 Voting Rights Act, black Americans began voting in large numbers. For the first time since Reconstruction, black Americans were elected to city, state and national government positions.

Black, White, Who's Right?

1. Black Americans have struggled for more than 350 years to enjoy basic human rights in housing, voting and education just as white Americans. Many Blacks feel that they have waited long enough. Some white Americans feel that black Americans are too impatient. They believe that change takes time and that black Americans should wait even longer. Who's right? Why?

_____

_____

_____

_____

2. Some black Americans feel that black and white Americans can live together in today's society in peace and harmony. Other black Americans feel that black and white Americans will never be able to live together in peace and harmony. Who's right? Why?

_____

_____

_____

_____

3. In the 1960's some black leaders such as Dr. Martin Luther King, Jr., believed that nonviolence was the best way to bring about changes in society. Other black Americans such as the Black Panthers felt that violence was the best way to change things. Who's right? Why?

_____

_____

_____

_____

4. Many white Americans joined black Americans in marches, sit-ins and other civil rights activities. Some even gave their lives in the struggle for black American rights. Some white Americans felt that these white Americans should not have participated in civil rights for black Americans. Who's right? Why?

_____

_____

_____

_____

Civil Rights Vocabulary

Listed below are some words that were used during the Civil Rights Era. Do you know the meanings of these words?

Word Bank

unconstitutional	integration	Black power
boycott	racist	patronize
segregation	freedom rides	abolish
sit-ins	demonstration	discrimination
Supreme Court	nonviolent	protest

Complete these sentences by filling the blanks with the correct words from the word bank.

Learn to spell each word in the word bank. Practice with a friend.

1. In 1955 Dr. Martin Luther King, Jr., led a bus _____ in Montgomery, Alabama.

2. The Civil Rights Act of 1968 forbade _____ by race in selling and renting of houses or apartments.

3. Dr. King believed that the _____ approach was the best way to change things.

4. In 1960 college students tested desegregation laws by asking to be served at lunch counters and restaurants. These were called _____ _____.

GA1345

5. In 1954 the Supreme Court ruled that separate schools were _____.

6. _____ is a word that means the separation of races or groups of people.

7. _____ means to combine or put together.

8. A person who believes that one race is superior to another is called a _____.

9. A _____ is a peaceful march.

10. In 1960 buses of black and white Americans made bus trips into the South to challenge civil rights laws. These trips were called _____ _____.

11. To get rid of something means to _____ it.

12. The _____ _____ made many civil rights decisions in the 1950's and 1960's.

13. If someone dislikes something, he/she could _____ it.

14. If you _____ a business, you buy its goods or services.

15. _____ _____ called for black Americans to band together and establish their own schools and businesses.

Black American Civil Rights Leaders

The struggle for civil rights began long before the 1950's and 1960's. As early as the 1800's courageous, brave and determined men and women dedicated themselves to the fight for freedom.

From Ida Wells Barnett (1869-1931) to Dr. Martin Luther King, Jr., (1929-1968) black Americans have given their time, talents and even their lives fighting discrimination and injustice. This span of years has produced many responsible and hardworking leaders. The last names of twenty of these leaders are hidden below. Can you find them? Use the names in the word list as your guide.

Word List

Ida Barnett	James Farmer	Eugene Jones	Channing Tobias
Daisy Bates	James Forman	Floyd McKissick	William Trotter
Montague Cobbs	Lester Granger	A. Phillip Randolph	Walter White
George Downing	Archibald Grimke	Mary Talbert	Roy Wilkins
W.E.B. Du Bois	Jesse Jackson	Mary Terrell	Whitney Young

```
G  N  I  N  W  O  D  A  J  J  G  T  T  U  K  R  Z  A  A  X  U
A  U  M  S  I  O  B  U  D  M  C  F  Q  Y  K  H  W  I  B  F  L
Q  D  A  C  L  D  E  N  G  O  D  P  P  Q  S  J  E  Z  M  Z  X
K  E  G  E  K  O  V  X  B  X  O  U  W  Z  H  H  F  L  C  Q  U
M  G  J  H  I  I  H  B  D  V  S  B  F  M  Y  Q  N  D  C  A  S
C  Y  O  U  N  G  S  D  V  T  W  L  D  D  J  O  Z  M  S  A  Y
G  D  N  D  S  N  L  S  W  Z  P  D  M  X  R  Q  A  Q  D  D  F
C  F  E  S  S  A  W  N  I  Z  R  O  T  I  O  F  O  U  H  H  P
V  P  S  D  A  M  C  A  I  C  C  Y  E  V  X  Y  E  S  V  W  B
U  E  K  M  I  R  G  W  S  I  K  W  C  U  U  L  R  R  N  Z  J
E  D  K  F  B  O  C  P  K  A  H  M  K  X  T  X  O  I  Q  S  Y
N  S  I  X  O  F  W  K  R  I  D  C  Y  K  I  Y  W  L  S  V  X
M  N  S  E  T  A  B  M  T  T  P  J  M  Z  R  O  P  Y  B  F  B
X  H  J  N  C  E  R  E  G  N  A  R  G  L  E  C  X  G  Q  A  Q
W  K  U  H  P  O  R  J  R  C  S  L  W  G  T  K  Q  B  R  R  T
Z  K  O  C  H  K  Q  R  K  K  Q  D  B  E  T  U  Y  N  V  M  S
F  G  I  W  Q  J  M  S  E  D  U  X  O  E  O  C  E  O  O  E  P
T  H  R  J  J  I  O  H  P  L  O  D  N  A  R  T  K  V  E  R  D
X  W  F  D  N  N  J  Y  O  S  L  L  V  I  T  T  S  P  G  U  U
```

Unscramble the circled letters to find the name of another great civil rights leader.

GA1345

Stepping-Stones

During the Civil Rights Era of the 1950's and 1960's, many events led to a better way of life for black Americans. Some of these events are written on the stepping-stones below. Cut out and arrange the stepping-stones along the freedom pathway in the correct order on page 225. When the stones are correctly arranged, they spell an important word for all Americans, especially black Americans.

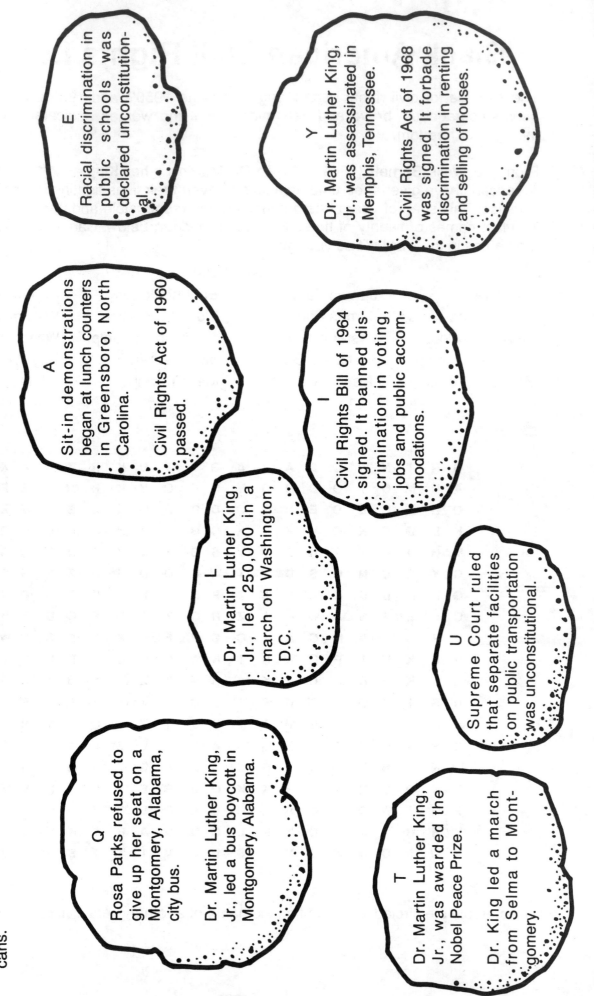

E
Racial discrimination in public schools was declared unconstitutional.

Y
Dr. Martin Luther King, Jr., was assassinated in Memphis, Tennessee.

Civil Rights Act of 1968 was signed. It forbade discrimination in renting and selling of houses.

A
Sit-in demonstrations began at lunch counters in Greensboro, North Carolina.

Civil Rights Act of 1960 passed.

I
Civil Rights Bill of 1964 signed. It banned discrimination in voting, jobs and public accommodations.

L
Dr. Martin Luther King, Jr., led 250,000 in a march on Washington, D.C.

U
Supreme Court ruled that separate facilities on public transportation was unconstitutional.

Q
Rosa Parks refused to give up her seat on a Montgomery, Alabama, city bus.

Dr. Martin Luther King, Jr., led a bus boycott in Montgomery, Alabama.

T
Dr. Martin Luther King, Jr., was awarded the Nobel Peace Prize.

Dr. King led a march from Selma to Montgomery.

GA1345

Freedom Pathway

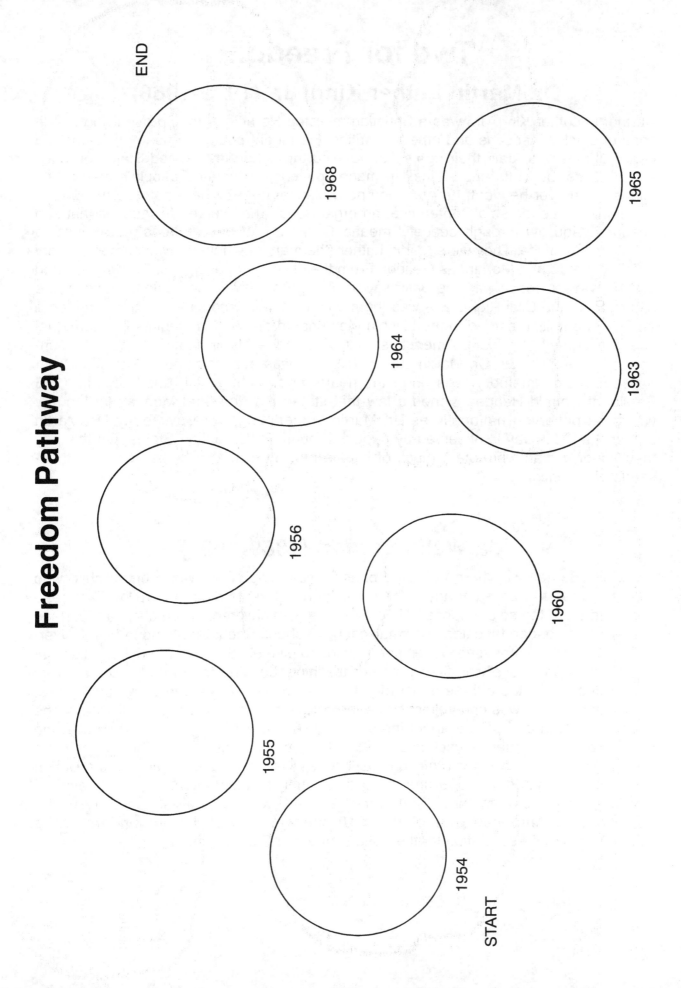

END

1968

1965

1964

1963

1956

1960

1955

1954

START

225

Two for Freedom

Dr. Martin Luther King, Jr. (1929-1968)

Dr. Martin Luther King, Jr., was a Christian minister. He helped to improve living conditions of black Americans and other minorities. He taught people to use nonviolent and peaceful means to gain their rights. He traveled throughout the United States organizing marches, boycotts and sit-ins. He made speeches to change people's hearts and minds. Wherever he went, he preached nonviolence. In 1957 he organized the Southern Christian Leadership Conference, an organization that worked for educational and economic equality through peaceful means. Dr. King had three heroes that helped to mold his way of life. They were Martin Luther (the man for whom he was named), Henry David Thoreau and Mohandas Gandhi. From their lives and teachings, Dr. King learned that nonviolent action was the best way to change old laws and customs. One of the highlights of the Civil Rights Era was the march on Washington in which Dr. King led a quarter of a million people to the Lincoln Memorial to demand immediate freedom, justice and equality for black Americans. There he made his famous "I Have a Dream" speech. In April 1968, Dr. Martin Luther King, Jr., was assassinated in Memphis, Tennessee. But his memory lives on in the hearts and minds of all Americans. In 1983 President Ronald Reagan signed a law that stated that the third Monday in January would be observed nationally as Dr. Martin Luther King, Jr., Day. Today Dr. Martin Luther King, Jr., Day is observed by people throughout the United States. On this day they honor a man who spent much of his life helping to make things better for thousands of Americans.

Ida Wells Barnett (1869-1931)

Ida Wells Barnett was born in Holly Springs, Mississippi. She was a bright child who learned to read at an early age. When both of her parents died in a yellow fever epidemic, Ida had the sole responsibility of raising seven children. When she was fourteen years old she bagan teaching in a small country school. She later attended Fisk University in Nashville, Tennessee. When she refused to give up her seat in a railroad car that said "whites only," she was fired from her teaching job. She then moved to Memphis, Tennessee. While there three of her friends were lynched. When she spoke out against the lynchings, she was compelled to flee the city. She went to Chicago. In Chicago she began speaking and writing about the awful injustice of lynching. She gathered all the records on the number of lynchings of black Americans in the South. The figures were staggering. She used this information in speeches that she made throughout the United States and England. In 1898 she led a delegation to Washington to see President McKinley to protest lynching. That same year she was appointed Secretary of the National Afro-American Council. In 1910 she was one of the cofounders of the NAACP–National Association for the Advancement of Colored People.

GA1345

King-Size Activity

Research the lives of each of Dr. King's heroes that helped to mold his life. Write the information beside each hero's picture.

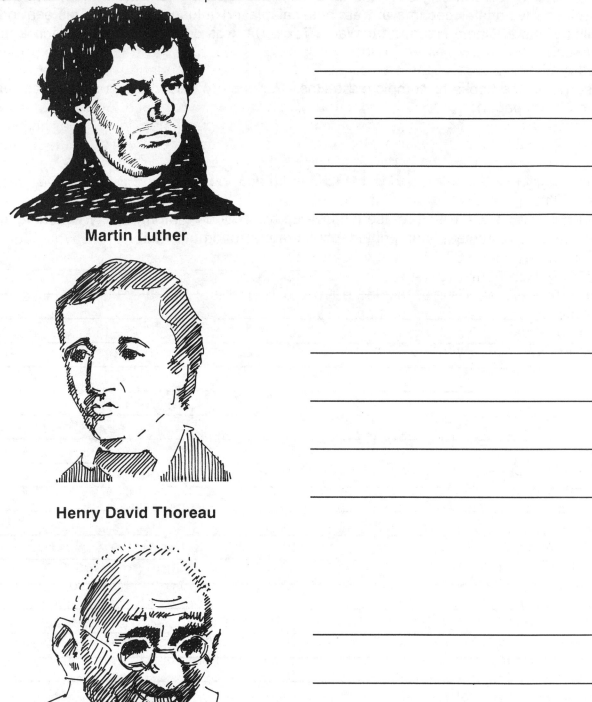

Martin Luther

_____

_____

_____

_____

Henry David Thoreau

_____

_____

_____

_____

Mohandas Gandhi

_____

_____

_____

_____

GA1345

The Rest of the Story

In the late 1800's when Ida Wells Barnett refused to give up her seat in a "whites only" section of a railroad car, she was fired from her teaching job. In 1944 when Jackie Robinson (who later became a great baseball player) refused to give up his seat on a military bus at Camp Hood, near Waco, Texas, he was court-martialed (tried in a military court).

Use reference books to complete the Rosa Parks story below (or on a sheet of notebook-sized paper).

The Rosa Parks Story

In 1955 when Rosa Parks refused to give up her seat on a Montgomery, Alabama, city bus, she was arrested, fingerprinted, photographed and put in jail.

_____

_____

_____

_____

_____

_____

_____

_____

_____

_____

_____

_____

_____

_____

_____

_____

_____

_____

_____

_____

_____

_____

GA1345

Real Heroes of the South

"One day," declared Dr. Martin Luther King, Jr., "the South will recognize its real heroes."

On Sunday, November 5, 1989, these prophetic words spoken by Dr. King came true. Families and friends of "the real heroes of the South" gathered near the Southern Poverty Law Center Building in Montgomery, Alabama, to dedicate a memorial to the forty brave men, women and children both white and black who were slain during the Civil Rights Movement between 1954 and 1968. Mrs. Rosa Parks spoke first. This was quite fitting, because her action in refusing to give up her seat and move to the back of the bus had started the modern Civil Rights Era. Then Julian Bond, a veteran civil rights worker, spoke. Members of the families of the slain victims spoke of the loss of their loved ones and the hurt and pain that they had experienced because of losing them.

The Civil Rights Memorial stands only a few blocks from the Montgomery State Capitol Building. Just behind it stands the Dexter Avenue Baptist Church where Dr. King preached and led his people in the civil rights struggle (the church has recently been named The King Memorial Baptist Church).

The memorial itself is a circular black table of granite stone. The names of the slain civil rights heroes and events of the Civil Rights Movement radiate from its center like the hands of a clock. Water emerges from an opening in the center of the table and spreads evenly and slowly across its face.

On a curved nine-foot wall behind the table are inscribed the often quoted words of Dr. Martin Luther King, Jr., taken from the biblical book of Amos..."Until justice rolls down like water and righteousness like a mighty stream." A thin sheet of water flows gently over the inscribed words.

Those who visit the memorial can touch the names of the slain heroes and see a reflection of themselves in its water. This is quite fitting because the Civil Rights Memorial was not built solely to honor the dead but also to remind the living of the history of the Civil Rights Movement.

Some of the names that appear on the memorial are well-known such as Dr. Martin Luther King, Jr., and Medgar Evers. Other names, such as Wharlest Jackson and white postal worker William Lewis Moore, are lesser known but all are "the real heroes of the South."

GA1345

Express Yourself

Write a poem expressing your thoughts about the Civil Rights Era. Dedicate your poem to the ones who gave their lives in the civil rights struggle. Use illustrations to make your poem more meaningful.

_____

_____

_____

_____

_____

_____

_____

_____

_____

Friendly Advice

You are the chairperson of the Committee for Better Race Relations in the United States. What advice can you give to each of the groups below that will cause a better, friendlier relationship?

Black Americans

_____

_____

_____

_____

White Americans

_____

_____

_____

_____

Answer Key

Unlock It! Page 2
1. auction
2. northern colonies
3. master
4. southern colonies
5. cotton gin
6. Black Codes
7. indentured servant
8. Africa
9. slaves
10. slave ownership

Place It, Page 7

14	4	7
2	10	12
15	11	9
1	3	13
6	5	8

Star Search, Page 13

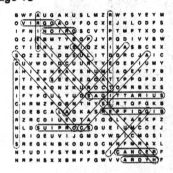

Answer, Please! Page 14
1. To help them bear the burden of hard work and long hours
2. "Go Down, Moses"
3. Big Dipper
4. "Swing Low, Sweet Chariot"
5. "Steal Away"

Decode It! Page 16
1. "Get on Board, Little Children"
2. "It's Me, Oh Lord"
3. "Deep River"
4. "Great Day"
5. "Couldn't Hear Nobody Pray"

The Original Thirteen, Page 24

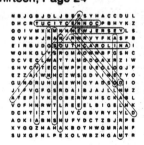

Where in the USA? Page 25

Battle Sheet, Page 27
1. Lexington, Concord; Massachusetts
2. Concord; Massachusetts
3. Ticonderoga; New York
4. Concord, Ticonderoga; Massachusetts, New York
5. Ticonderoga; New York
6. Great Bridge; Virginia
7. Concord; Bunker Hill; Massachusetts
8. Ticonderoga; New York
9. Concord, Massachusetts
10. Bunker Hill; Massachusetts
11. Yorktown; Virginia
12. Concord; Massachusetts

Seaman, Soldier or Spy, Page 30
1. Sp
2. So
3. So
4. So
5. So
6. So
7. So
8. So
9. So, Sp
10. So
11. Se

1. carrot
2. red
3. in
4. stop
5. puppy
6. United
7. salt
8. apple
9. truck
10. top
11. up
12. cold
13. cake
14. six

Crispus Attucks

Search and Supply, Page 34

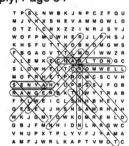

1. Oliver
2. James
3. Crispus
4. Tack
5. William
6. Seymour
7. James
8. James
9. Caesar
10. Edward
11. Peter
12. Barzillai
13. Saul
14. Prince
15. Lemuel
16. Joseph
17. Salem

We Believe, Page 47
1. Slavery was wrong and all persons living in the United States should have freedom and equal rights.
2. Slavery could be abolished by appealing to the people and telling them that slavery was wrong.
3. Slavery could be abolished by electing politicians who opposed slavery so they could pass laws abolishing slavery.
4. Guerrilla warfare was the best way to end slavery.
5. Black Americans and women should have the same rights as any other person.

GA1345

Chain of Events, Page 48
1785–The beginning of the Abolition Era
1831–Garrison published the first Abolition newspaper.
1837–Elijah Lovejoy was killed because he printed anti-slavery articles in his newspaper.
1852–Harriet Beecher Stowe wrote *Uncle Tom's Cabin*.
1859–John Brown used guerrilla warfare in an attempt to abolish slavery.

Name That Man, Page 52
1. James McCune Smith
2. Henry Highland Garnet
3. Charles Lenox Remond
4. Samuel Cornish
5. Robert Purvis
6. James Forten
7. William Still
8. Theodore S. Wright
9. William Whipple
10. James W.C. Pennington

Math-Age-Matics, Page 53

1. 67	3. 69	5. 81	7. 61	9. 50
2. 63	4. 88	6. 80	8. 76	10. 52

11. Robert Purvis   12. Theodore S. Wright

Life Signs, Page 56
1817–He was born.
1841–Spoke at an antislavery meeting
1847–Returned to New York and began publishing his newspaper, *The North Star*
1863–Organized two regiments of black soldiers
1874–Became president of the Freedman's Saving and Trust Company
1877–Became a United States Marshal
1880–Appointed Recorder of Deeds for Washington, D.C.
1889–Became American Consul-General to Haiti
1895–Frederick Douglass died.

Secrets (Part 2), Page 59
1. safety of travel
2. escaping slaves
3. food and clothing
4. send slaves on to the next station
5. change directions
6. secret places
7. escaping slaves

What's Happening? Page 76
2. Maine applied for admission to the Union.
3. The Missouri Compromise
4. Gold was discovered in California.
5. Bitter debate arose in Congress.
6. Henry Clay proposed a solution to the problem between the northern and southern states.
7. The Compromise of 1850
8. Northerners became angry.
9. Personal liberty laws were passed.
10. The nation was headed for a civil war.

The Lineup, Page 82
Confederate states: Alabama, Arkansas, Florida, Georgia, Louisiana, Mississippi, North Carolina, South Carolina, Tennessee, Texas, Virginia
Border states: Delaware, Kentucky, Maryland, Missouri

Find the Winners, Page 87

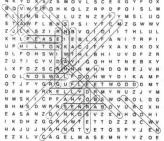

1. Christian
2. James
3. William
4. John
5. Decatur
6. Joachin
7. Miles
8. Robert
9. Aaron
10. James
11. Milton
12. Alfred
13. William
14. Robert
15. Powhatan
16. Edward
17. Wilson
18. Thomas
19. James
20. William
21. Alexander
22. Charles

Facts and Figures of the Civil War, Page 88
1. 31,443,000
2. 4,441,000
3. 3,500,000
4. 22,000,000
5. 9,000,000
6. 200,000
7. 186,000;133,000
8. 30,000
9. 800,000
10. 450,000

College Completion, Page 109
2. 1867; Raleigh, North Carolina; Coeducational
3. 1869; Tougaloo, Mississippi; Coeducational
4. 1868; Hampton, Virginia; Coeducational
5. 1865; Raleigh, North Carolina; Coeducational
6. 1867; Washington, D.C.; Coeducational
7. 1869; Atlanta, Georgia; Coeducational
8. 1867; Altanta, Georgia; Men
9. 1866; Nashville, Tennessee; Coeducational

Respond, Please..., Page 123
1. South Carolina
2. All served three terms in Congress, all from South Carolina
3. Joseph Rainey and Robert Smalls
4. South Carolina
5. Hiram Revels and Blanche Bruce
6. Mississippi
7. Florida, Virginia, Louisiana
8. North Carolina
9. Benjamin Sterling Turner, James Rapier, Jeremiah Haralson
10. Josiah T. Wells

Young's Ladder of Success, Page 139
1864–Birth
1884–Appointed to attend U.S. Military Academy at West Point
1889–Graduated from Military Academy
1894–Instructor of military science at Wilberforce University
1898–Appointed a major in Spanish-American War
1915–Commanded Tenth Cavalry
1917–U.S. entered World War I. Young was not assigned to European service.
1922–Went to Nigeria to gather material for a book

GA1345

Freedom Forest, Page 172

1. NAACP	4. CORE
2. NUL	5. SCLC
3. ASALH	6. SNCC

Outstanding Achievers in Black History, Page 175

1. 1915
2. Ernest E. Just
3. 1938
4. the first black Americans to attend Central High School in Little Rock, Arkansas
5. Marian Anderson
6. 1957
7. Henry (Hank) Aaron
8. twelve
9. Mordecai Johnson, Henry A. Hunt, Robert R. Moton, William T.B. Williams, Mary McLeod Bethune, John Hope, Charles H. Houston, Wilson C. Riles, Rayford W. Logan, Benjamin E. Mays, Bill Cosby, Frederick Patterson
10. eight
11. W.S. Braithwaite, Archibald H. Grimke, James Weldon Johnson, Charles W. Chestnutt, Richard Wright, Langston Hughes, Gordon Parks, Alex Haley
12. Robert C. Weaver, Edward W. Brooke, Coleman Young, Thomas Bradley, Percy S. Sutton
13. George Washington Carver
14. She started the Civil Rights Movement by refusing to give up her seat to a white passenger on a Montgomery, Alabama, city bus.
15. He became known for his research on blood preservation and for the organization of blood banks
16. Answers will vary.

Complete a Cycle, Page 177

1. Factories began to produce more goods.
2. Many people were laid off work.
3. Without jobs people did not have money to buy goods.
4. Goods piled up in stores.

Tell It Like It Was, Page 180

1. They died of diseases, hunger and exposure as they hitchhiked across the country looking for jobs.
2. They suffered from deficiency diseases such as rickets and pellagra.
3. Teachers fed over 10,000 hungry school children on their skimpy salaries.
4. They marched on the nation's capital because they did not get a promised bonus.
5. They shined shoes for a nickel.
6. They slept in freight train cars and traveled across the country looking for jobs.
7. People slept on park benches in city parks.
8. They shot their animals because they did not bring enough at the market.
9. They stayed home because their parents could not afford to buy clothing for them.
10. They were producing too many products which could not be sold, so many sharecroppers were without jobs.

Help! Help! Page 182

1. increased farm income
2. controlled flooding and provided electricity along the Tennessee River
3. helped young men find work on conservation projects
4. provided electricity for farm homes
5. created jobs through the building of public places, such as schools, courthouses, bridges, etc.
6. created jobs for artists, writers, actors and musicians as well as other needy people
7. provided pensions for the aged
8. insured loan companies against loss on home mortgage loans
9. regulated radio, telephone and telegraph systems
10. insured bank deposits

The Black Cabinet, Page 185

1. Robert Vann	7. Lester Walton
2. Edgar Brown	8. Ira Reid
3. Mary McCleod Bethune	9. Ambrose Caliver
4. Robert C. Weaver	10. Eugene Jones
5. Walter White	11. Frank Horne
6. Ralph Bunche	12. Lawrence Oxley

Help Symbols, Page 187

1. SSB	4. WPA	7. CCC
2. WPA	5. REA	8. NYA
3. AAA	6. TVA	9. FSA

Proper Placement, Page 189

Actors: Ethel Waters, Richard Harrison, Paul Robeson
Composers: Duke Ellington, William Dawson
Novelists: Richard Wright

Who's Who? Page 192

1. J.L.	3. J.O.	5. J.O.	7. J.L.	9. J.O.
2. J.L.	4. J.L.	6. J.L.	8. J.O.	10. J.L.

1. football	8. basketball	15. football
2. baseball	9. baseball	16. baseball
3. football	10. boxing	17. basketball
4. tennis	11. track	18. football
5. boxing	12. basketball	19. baseball
6. baseball	13. baseball	20. boxing
7. tennis	14. boxing	

Awards and Achievements ..., Page 195

1. Benjamin O. Davis, Jr.; Charles Gandy
2. Vernon Baker
3. Benjamin O. Davis, Jr.
4. Benjamin O. Davis, Jr.; Albert F. William
5. Norman Day
6. Benjamin O. Davis, Jr.
7. W.P. Terrell, Steve Rodriguez, Ernest Jenkins, George Edwards, Arthur Jackson

GA1345

Doing More, Page 197

1. Purple Heart
2. Distinguished Service Cross
3. Medal of Honor (Navy, Air Force, Army)
4. Navy Cross
5. Bronze Star
6. Silver Star
7. Air Force Cross
8. Commendation Medal (Navy, Army, Coast Guard, Air Force)
9. Distinguished Service Medal (Army, Navy, Coast Guard, Air Force)
10. Air Medal
11. Airman's Medal
12. Soldier's Medal
13. Distinguished Flying Cross
14. Navy and Marine Corps Medal
15. Legion of Merit
16. Defense Distinguished Service Medal

Let's Organize, Page 199

10, 1, 5, 2, 6, 4, 7, 3, 8, 9

James' Things, Page 204

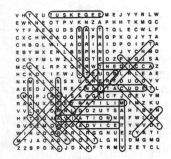

First Matches, Page 210

1. Marian Anderson
2. Althea Gibson
3. Wilma Randolph
4. Sidney Poitier
5. Shirley Chisholm
6. Jackie Robinson
7. Thurgood Marshall
8. Gwendolyn Brooks
9. Patricia Harris
10. Robert C. Weaver
11. Ralph Bunche
12. Edward Brooke
13. Andrew Brimmer
14. Constance Motley
15. Andrew Young

Thurgood Marshall

Whose Pen? Page 214

1. Richard Wright
*2. Charles Gordone
*3. Gwendolyn Brooks
*4. Toni Morrison
5. Chester Hines
6. Frank Yerby
7. Ann Petry
8. William Motley
9. James Baldwin
10. Ralph Ellison
11. Eldridge Cleaver
*12. Alex Haley
13. Lorraine Hansberry
14. Alice Walker
*15. August Wilson
16. Nikki Giovanni
17. Langston Hughes
18. Richard Wright
19. James Baldwin
20. LeRoi Jones (Imamu Amiri Baraka)

Civil Rights Vocabulary, Pages 221-222

1. boycott
2. discrimination
3. nonviolent
4. sit-ins
5. unconstitutional
6. Segregation
7. Integration
8. racist
9. demonstration
10. freedom rides
11. abolish
12. Supreme Court
13. protest
14. patronize
15. Black power

Black American Civil Rights Leaders, Page 223

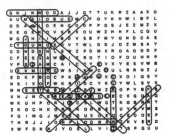

Dr. Martin Luther King, Jr.

Freedom Pathway, Page 225

EQUALITY

GA1345